Secrets of
Decision Island

Secrets of Decision Island

A Framework for Making Good Decisions

Tom Berryhill

ETI PUBLISHING

Expression Technology Inc.

Vancouver, Canada

ISBN: 978-0-9948071-3-7

Book and cover design by Tom Berryhill

First paperback printing, September 2015

Contents

Introduction

When you face an important decision, it seems to be always on your mind. You go through your day normally, but you can feel a little detached from the world. People close to you may ask if everything is okay. They detect a slight change in your focus. If you trust them, you might let them in on what is distracting you. If they have experience in the area, you might consider their thoughts and advice. You take them into your "inner circle" for this decision. As you make progress, you check in with them again. The rest of the world is going on normally while you, with your inner circle, feel somewhat separate. This is your "Decision Island."

I have seen people struggle under pressure from the importance of a looming decision. The struggle for many is the lack of a framework in which to consider their choices. Emotion enters their process along with pressure, and certain choices change their appeal. Choices can become more attractive or more upsetting as emotion takes hold. Feelings towards choices can overtake a fair-minded study.

It has made me wonder, "Would we give more thought to our choices if we had a simple framework for making decisions?"

If we could follow a process for decisions that lets us use our feelings as part of the solution, could we make better decisions? I know some older people who are happy with their lives. They tell me that even though they have experienced some awful situations, they were always glad they made the decisions they did. They thought about their decisions, but they also honoured their feelings. They figured out how to make choices for personal progress and feel good about it. When I ask them if happiness is a goal in their lives, they say it is not. It comes to them spontaneously through fruitful achievement.

I have also known people who have made some bad decisions in their life. Many of them seem to continue making bad decisions. It's almost as if they can't help it. Happiness is not as familiar to them as is trying to cope. Some have told me that they don't really think much about making decisions. They prefer to "do" than to "think."

Since we all have free will, isn't it better to use it with some responsibility to ourselves? Don't we owe it to ourselves to make good decisions? Those who make good decisions seem much happier. They enjoy life and are great to be around.

If people started trying to make good decisions at a younger age, would they be able to use that as a skill throughout their life? Certainly, learning it later in life seems a little tougher. Could you use a simple framework for looking at decision choices? Younger people might use it to help them simplify complex situations. If they got good at it, they could do it easily in their mind. Whenever they faced a tough decision, they could fall back on the framework they mastered when they were young. This could help them make better choices. Such a framework might help people of any age. If you used it, you would at least have a new way to talk with others about decisions.

This book presents a simple framework for decision-making that you can also expand for more challenging decisions. It reveals steps and processes to make the merits of choices more obvious to you. It gives you a way of talking clearly about your choices and your regard for them. It helps you work with your trusted inner circle of people without feeling too isolated on your "Decision Island." You will discover "secret tips" all along the way, to help you make better decisions. They can help guide you to a way of life that values good decisions.

Whatever stage of life you are in, I hope you find value in this book. If you are a teen or young adult, please know that I wrote this book with you in mind. I hope you are able to try the process and become good at it. At the very least, if you start thinking more about your choices, you will start bringing more purpose to your life.

Chapter 1

Why Think About Decisions?

If you make good decisions, you have a much greater chance of living the kind of life you want. If you consistently make bad decisions, you increase the negative drama in your life and feel out of control. Pick one. That's right; it's a decision. Can we actually choose to make good decisions? What do you think? Is decision-making a skill that we can learn, practice and develop? As we make more and more good decisions, are we improving the skills that help us make good decisions? If we're always making bad decisions, are we falling into a habit of ignoring consequences? Can we avoid bringing unnecessary challenges into our lives?

Significant Decisions

In the heat of the moment, it's easy to take action that you will always regret. Just before that action, you make a momentary decision, ignoring its significance. Ignoring the significance of a decision is often disastrous. Pausing to consider the significance of a decision is the first step towards improving its quality, and its outcome.

We make so many decisions every day. For many of them, we are repeating well-established patterns that we choose to follow on that particular day. We create those patterns by performing the steps repeatedly, as if in a play. At first, we carefully choose those steps to produce the desired outcome. Then they become predictable behaviours that we value to simplify our lives.

Other behaviours are responses to unique situations that arise to our surprise. In a split second, our brain provides an impulse to react to the new stimulus. This quick reaction ability we have can save us from immanent harm, or mild discomfort. While a reaction like that can be quite significant for our protection, we give it little thought beforehand. It comes from a part of our brain that does not get involved in thoughtful consideration. If something makes a sudden loud sound, your muscles jump and you look towards the sound. With a lot of mental effort, you can override that behaviour and keep your cool. That is training.

Can we train ourselves to recognize the significance of a decision before just reacting? If we can, we will move from being buffeted by surrounding events to following a path that we decide to pursue. To begin that training, we need to consider time-frame. It is much easier to train ourselves to pause and consider the significance of a decision when we have the luxury of time to ponder. Developing our ability in those situations sets up a pattern of considering our choice of action. It lays the groundwork for thinking quickly on our feet and still getting the desired results.

So let's start by focusing on decisions where time is not a big issue. Assessing the significance of an upcoming decision helps us to focus attention on what matters most. While it does involve a little bit of thinking ahead, it's worth it. Important decisions often have a huge affect on you or those you care about. If you find yourself wondering for a while about a decision's affect, it is likely to be a significant decision. Thinking that a decision is not important when it is can be a big mistake.

Considered Decisions

Are "considered" decisions the best decisions? Not always, but significant decisions that are not considered properly are a hit-and-miss game. You're dealing with the odds in that case. What are the odds that a person who goes through life without considering the decisions they make will have a life they enjoy? On the other hand, you can give great thought to a major life decision and still later wish you had made a different choice. Of course, in that case, we typically rationalize and focus on the benefits of the choice we did make. If you are happy with outcomes you didn't expect, you are still happy. In making decisions though, it is best to try for the outcome we desire.

Being able to see farther down a path often helps us align our choices with a future we desire. Imagining what it will be like to live with a decision, helps us resolve our feelings. We can compare how we feel in that imaginary scenario to how we would like to feel in the future. That is the essence of considering a decision. We take the steps in our mind and pretend that we are experiencing it as our new reality. It's a thought experiment. We conduct it in the safe environment of our mind, so we can feel free to make huge mistakes. All we have to do is recognize them as such, and then change our choices in the experiment.

Secret Tip: **Imagine how you would feel living with your decision in the future.**

Good and Bad Decisions

What is a good decision for one person, group, or team can be a bad decision for others. This is clear on the sports playing field. Scoring the next goal directs every decision on your team. When all the decisions succeed in scoring the goal, your team members agree that the decisions were good. The disappointed opposing team members feel that those same decisions were bad for them. But they must admit that, as decision-making goes, you made victorious decisions.

This illustrates two points about the quality of decisions. First, revealing the true merits of a decision requires you to carry out the decision. Second, a good decision helps to achieve a goal for the decision-maker. So that means you should have a clear goal in mind before trying to make your decision.

Secret Tip: **You see the true merits of a decision after it is made.**

Secret Tip: **Clarify your goal before making a choice.**

How can we know beforehand whether making a decision a certain way will be good? We can't know for sure, but we can make an "educated guess," also known as an informed decision. Experience is a great educator. If you have made a good decision many times before in similar situations, you are well informed to make the decision again. For new decisions, learning more about the situation helps us predict the affect the decision will have. It may also let us spot any unexpected outcomes. The goal here is to improve your "confidence level" in making the decision. It helps you to be more "sure" about your choice.

With new information, we can simulate the implementation of a decision in our minds. We can use our thought experiment and explore the ramifications. Imagine how it affects others, opens doors for us, and closes other doors. Does the decision cost us resources such as money or a commitment of time, or bring us new options and new resources. By immersing ourselves in that potential environment, we can judge whether the decision was a good or bad decision. It could even be neither, but be the best decision under the circumstances. By trying to do this as much as we can in our minds, we are exercising and preparing to be ready when we make a final decision and act on it.

After we make a bad decision, we must live with the consequences. How well we accept responsibility for that bad decision will determine the degree to which we will learn from it.

Reflection and Anticipation

It can be hard to accept responsibility personally for a bad decision we have made. Think of one you have made. If you had a chance to do it over again, would you make the same decision? Knowing what you now know, perhaps not. But what about the next time you're facing a tough decision? What can you learn from this decision, now that it has turned out to be a bad one? What new rule can you set out for yourself that will alert you in the future to avoid the mistake made here? Don't be rash when proclaiming the rule; be reasonable. We need something that will likely work without hindering us from moving towards the opportunities we want.

When we immediately reflect on a bad decision, we may tend to go a bit overboard in our resolution to avoid future mistakes. "I will never again listen to anything that person says." Well, maybe that's a good decision, but perhaps it's a bit of an overreaction. In the future, when you get information from that person, will you trust it? Maybe you'll "take it with a grain of salt." You might even seek some corroboration of those facts from some other source. But look at you! You are already making new rules about how you will go about decision-making in the future. You are learning from your mistakes. That's growth.

Can we learn from good decisions too? We often tend to just celebrate and move on. Perhaps we should pause and identify the critical things we did that resulted in that choice. When you have a moment, reflect, analyse, and recognize what you did. Try to be honest with yourself. Reinforce in your mind those things you did that helped you make a good decision. Honour those steps; they worked. Be ready to call upon the experience you just gained when you face a similar experience in the future.

The more you reflect on your decisions, the more you are training yourself to make good decisions. Your recent increase in perspective and experience suggests how you might improve future decisions.

Secret Tip: **Reflecting on a recent decision can help you improve future decisions.**

Chapter 2

Understanding Decisions

So what makes up a decision? It's a thought process that results in some sort of action. Not all actions are due to decisions, but considered actions usually have a lot of thought behind them. Why all that thought? Why think about it? Why not just do it? The simple answer is, "Because of the consequences."

You and your friends are hiking and come up to the top of a cliff, with water some 20 feet down below. It's a hot day and you are all thinking about a swim. None of you has seen this water hole before, and there are no signs that others have used it for swimming. The idea of diving or jumping into the water comes up, as an alternative to climbing down to it. What are you thinking about? Why not just do it? You start thinking about risk. Is it a 20-foot drop into three feet of water? Could there be big rocks submerged below the surface? Do you have enough information to make a good decision? What are your options?

Making a good decision can involve asking a lot of questions. Making a bad decision may not involve asking any questions at all, at least not *before* the decision. Questions are a convenient way to gather missing information, identify options and explore alternatives. If you decide to go ahead with a decision before you have all the relevant answers, risks increase. That poses another question: are the rewards worth the risk? It can seem like a complex decision. Let's try to simplify it.

Seeing Simple Decisions

Is there such a thing as a simple decision? Some are simpler than others. If you think about a simple decision long enough, you should be able to turn it into a complex decision. That's sort of a ridiculous thought, but it identifies a spectrum. You can add complexity to a decision by mentally exploring highly unlikely consequences. Risk can seem inflated when you stay ignorant of the facts. These two factors will help you sift through the complexity: risk and likelihood.

The best goal is to reduce complex decisions to simple ones. Let's try reversing the logic above for our two factors, risk and likelihood. We can reduce complexity by answering questions with facts, and expose the risks for what they are. Knowing more about the risks, we then focus on the big risks. They usually have big consequences. We can further reduce complexity by considering the likelihood of each risk. If we have a good understanding of the risks and their likelihood, the decision becomes simpler. We dismiss all the unlikely small risks. Then we focus on the likely big risks.

We can also simplify a complex decision by considering its parts. We may be able to see several other easier decisions inside it. When we become familiar with these, other parts of the decision may be easier to grasp. Decisions can also seem complex because of their vast range of choices. By using examples of likely choices, we can reduce the range while we ponder. We can build a smaller set of distinct choices to help us better understand the issue. Then we can tailor our response to just those choices and help clarify our position.

Writing a list of possible choices can help simplify your decision process. When you start focusing on one choice's details, glimpsed choices could distract you and lurk in the back of your mind. By creating the list, you can free up your mind to think of other possible choices. What are all the possible choices you could make for this decision? Staying at that level in your mind seems to make it easier to think about the decision.

Secret Tip: **Start to simplify a decision by writing a list of possible choices.**

Risks and Benefits

Each choice has its risks and benefits. But which choice will be a good decision? Would you agree that a good decision lets you achieve the benefits while tolerating the risks? To understand a risk better, we need to imagine it. That can be hard to face, but important to do. Think of a significant decision you made in your past, or one you are now facing. Pick one choice and try writing down a label for each of the major risks. There may be several. Labelling a risk lets you summarize it into a phrase. You can use that label to think about the risk, and talk to others about it. When we think about a particular risk, we tend to feel its strength. Is it a big risk or a small one? For each risk, try to express its strength with a number. You could use a scale of 1 to 10, and write that number next to the risk label.

Secret Tip: **Label each risk so you can think and**
                talk about it more easily with others.

Along with each risk, consider its likelihood based on facts, not fear. How likely is that risk to occur if you follow through with that choice? We know that if the risk does occur, it will be big or small as you have said, but what are the chances that it will happen? Try to express that likelihood on a scale of 1 to 10, and write that number next to the risk strength. So now, we have a choice with risks, and each risk has a number for strength and a number for likelihood.

Let's describe the benefits for this choice. That's usually easy to do. Wasn't the reason you came up with this choice was because of its benefit? Perhaps it's an alternate choice as in, "Well, I could always do that." List all the major benefits you can see by using a label to describe them. Let's also confirm the importance to you of each benefit. Is it a big benefit? You can use the same 1 to 10 scale to rate the strength of the benefit. Finally, confirm the likelihood of each benefit. Yes, that would be a huge benefit, but how likely is it to happen? Think of it on a scale of 1 to 10 and write that number next to the number for benefit strength.

Now you have a concise chart to help inform you about your decision. You have listed risks and benefits for the first choice, both with likelihoods. That alone can be a great help, but you have more. You have the seriousness of each risk and the importance of each benefit.

In *Figure 1* below, Kayla is considering a job offer she received after applying in several cities. This one came from a distant city. She has been away from home before, but not for long. This would mean moving to the new city. She is trying to make sense of how she feels about this job offer.

#	Choice	Risk	Strength	Likelihood	Benefit	Strength	Likelihood
1	Accept Offer	miss home	5	6	Learn a lot	8	10
					earn some $$	9	8
					New friends	7	6

Figure 1

Let's look at the most likely risks and benefits for *your* choice. How likely are they? Did they score above a six? Let's focus on the ones with a likelihood of six or more. How important are those benefits to you? Are they attractive? Did your most important benefit make it into the "most likely" group? If not, could you take steps to improve the likelihood of acquiring that benefit? Let's consider the most likely risk. How serious is it? Are you concerned about any of the most likely risks? Could you mitigate, or soften the effect of their consequences somehow? Could you help your environment adapt to the decision you are about to make? Are there things you could do to help you accept the risk?

One value of a chart is that it brings an internal concept out into the open. It is no longer a vague idea with lots of moving parts in your mind. It becomes tangible, so you can touch it and discuss it. Showing someone how you view your decision choices will help you both discuss them and gain the other's perspective.

You use the thinking part of your mind to choose numbers for your view of risk and benefit. This can help you get another perspective on an emotional situation. Some people like working with numbers. If you are discussing your decision with a person like that, telling them your numbers will help them grasp your view of the situation.

Secret Tip: **Chart your decision choices to make them clear to you and others.**

If you are a visual person who prefers to *see* what numbers mean, you can visualize your numbers this way. Think of your risk as a dial, like a speedometer with a needle or a line pointing to the left. The bigger the risk, the higher the needle arcs upwards. For a risk of 10, the needle looks like a line straight up. For a smaller risk, the needle arcs up only a little. For Kayla, the risk was five, as shown in *Figure 2*. *Likelihood* shows as the length of the needle to a maximum of 10. Kayla's risk had a likelihood of six.

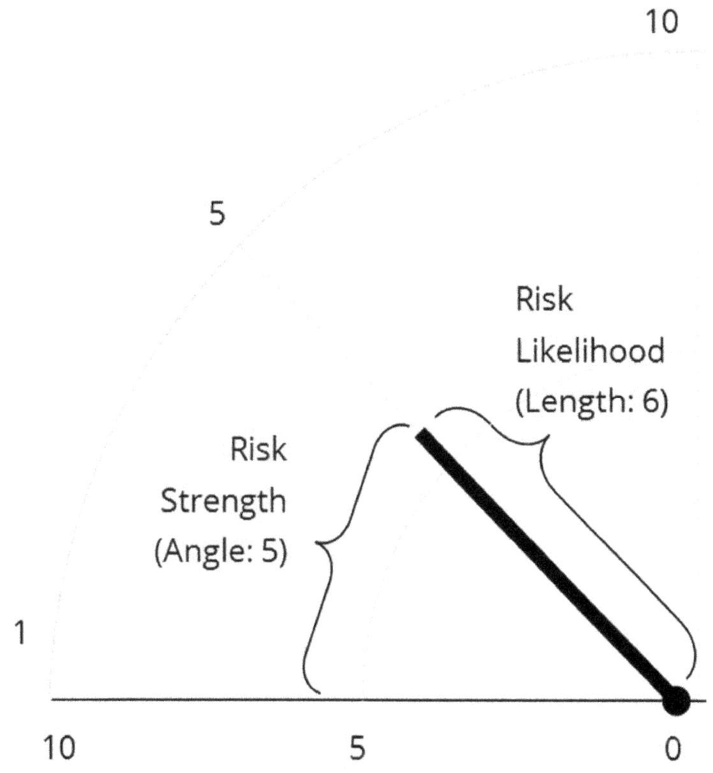

Figure 2

Looking at *Figure 2*, we see that the angle represents the strength of the risk, and the length of the line shows how likely it is. We could have a long, almost horizontal line. That would show a very small risk that is certain to happen, like a small cost. We could also think of a huge risk that is quite unlikely. It would show as a very short line, extending straight up. Using the speedometer metaphor, the faster you go the more risk you have. The likelihood of that risk is the length of the line.

If you like this visual way of thinking about the numbers for risk strength and likelihood, we can apply a similar visual to benefit. We use the angle of the line to represent the *strength* of risk or benefit. Benefit lines rotate from the right side, counter-clockwise towards the top. We use the length of the line to represent the *likelihood* of the risk or benefit.

For Kayla, her only risk was "miss home," and her biggest benefit was to "earn some $$." *Figure 3* shows these together. That benefit strength was 9, and the likelihood was 8. So, the benefit angle at 9 would almost, but not quite, be straight up. The likelihood at 8 would not reach, but come near the top. After drawing the strongest risk and benefit, we can fill in the chart with the others. Kayla had three benefits, and only one risk.

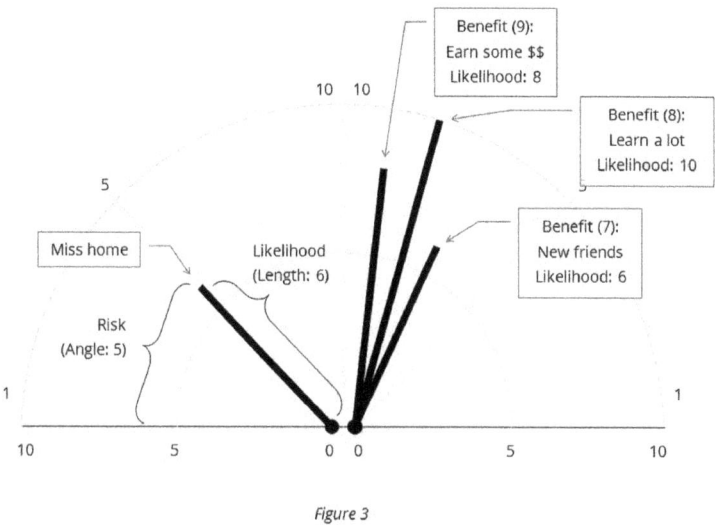

Figure 3

By just glancing at *Figure 3,* we see this to be an outstanding choice for Kayla. She needs to compare it with her other choices, but this visual representation can help her do that.

You might consider diagramming the choices for your next significant decision. Some of the people you ask to help you think through your decision may prefer to see the diagram instead of just the numbers. If you would like a more rigorous visual approach that uses building blocks instead of angles, please see the section at the end of this book, called *An Alternate Visual Model.*

Regardless of whether you prefer to create a chart of the numbers, a diagram of the choices, or both, these form the basis of our decision framework. Even if you don't always write them down, thinking about your choices in this way can help you get perspective on your decision options.

Pros and Cons

Simple decisions can be yes/no. Either you do it or you don't. It is a basic choice, although it may not seem easy to make. Some decisions though, involve choosing one out of *many* possibilities. Just pick one. But the risks, benefits, and likelihoods all just multiplied. Each choice option carries its own set of characteristics. You might also have mixed feelings about each option's benefits. This could get complicated, so you might want to use a simpler method.

With multiple-choice decisions, it is easier to use a pros and cons approach. For each option to choose from, make a list of factors in favour (pro) of that choice and other factors against (con) that choice. Pro factors include benefits, its importance, your desire for it, and any other things in its favour. Con factors include risks, consequences, unimportance, and any other things against it.

Look at the pro and con list and see if one choice ranks higher in the pros and lower in the cons than the others. This is a subjective analysis, so you should get facts to confirm the data. Even if one choice does not stand out from the others, you have a chart that you can show someone to help gain their perspective. Often, pros and cons provide a good place to start looking at a decision. If this simple approach doesn't seem sufficient to help you analyse your choices, you can move on to a more detailed look at risk and benefit. This framework we are building also includes some shortcuts that might help you decide quickly.

Getting Another Opinion

It can be worthwhile to have someone else understand your situation and give you an opinion. The value comes from being able to see your situation from their point of view. If you ask for their opinion before you have facts about your situation, you can only discuss a hypothetical situation. Without facts, they are guessing what they would do. Any advice they give you is a guess. If you get facts later that do not support your initial guess, their advice is no longer valuable.

By looking into your situation before you ask the opinions

and advice of others, you can help ensure you get better advice. You can tell the people what you have found out and what you know. They will realize you have looked into the facts of the matter and will take your questions more seriously. If they give you advice, they will base it on your actual situation instead of an imagined possibility.

Secret Tip: **Investigate your situation's facts before asking the opinions of others.**

You do need to choose the *right* person to give you an opinion. Ensuring they are the right person almost needs its own pro and con list. To narrow this down, let's again try a ridiculous thought. What if you posted your decision chart on social media and had the whole world give you their opinion on what you should do? While you take your situation seriously, do you know of any people who might use it for their entertainment? Have you heard people gossip about dilemmas that other people are facing? Have you seen people make fun of serious situations? What kind of "advice" would come from them? So maybe we should share with only the right people.

The right people will form our trusted "inner-circle" that we can confide in. In a sense, we are bringing them onto our

Decision Island. We will trust them not to share our situation with the whole world, and keep it to themselves until we decide. We want to keep this process confidential and shield ourselves from outside pressures. Once we decide, we will act on it and likely let everyone know what we are doing. Until then, this is the real secret of our Decision Island.

Finding the right person to give you an opinion can be a challenge. You want a person who makes good decisions. That means that they are already successful in what they do. But maybe they became successful using methods that you don't respect. So you want their values to be similar, or at least aligned with yours. You also want them to be familiar with your subject, so they can relate to the risks and benefits. So to sum up, they should be knowledgeable about your subject, and successful with similar values.

If you ask a person like that for their opinion on your pending decision, they are likely going to be glad to help. They will recognize that you have done your "homework" and are serious about your analysis of the situation. Once they give you their perspective and opinion, it will affect your perspective too. You chose this person carefully. It's not like an opinion from someone who is joking around (stay away from those).

If your own opinion differs from this person's opinion or recommendation, don't give up. Get a second opinion. It could be possible that they have a hidden agenda influencing their advice. Carefully select another advisor. After they weigh in, and your opinion differs from both of theirs, pause to consider. In the end, it is your decision. Even though it looks like your opinion is in the minority, it could be a risk you need to take. If it turns out to be a bad decision, you can learn from that. Of course, it will only be worth the risk if the risk is small. For large-risk decisions, get a third opinion and try to be open to persuasion from those you trust. But, it is your life, so it is your decision.

Secret Tip: **Seek help from knowledgeable people who are successful and share your values.**

Consequences and Opportunities

Identifying risks and benefits is great for putting labels on the key issues of a decision. But the consequences of those risks, and opportunities presented by the benefits, tell the real story. When we describe the consequences, we get a better understanding of a risk. When we list the possible opportunities presented by a choice, we see the importance of a benefit more clearly. Once again, it is essential to associate likelihood with these projections. Most of our attention should go to the most likely possibilities. We can explore the most likely consequences of a risk and imagine what we would do if they happened. How would we cope? What could we do ahead of time to prepare for a particular consequence? Playing it out in your mind can reveal new options for you.

New opportunities are among the benefits gained from making a decision. This is usually our motivation for making that choice. But how should we best use these new opportunities? We can imagine facing those opportunities to see what we would do. What would happen if we pursued an opportunity in a certain way?

As you can see, anticipating both consequences and opportunities raises new questions. It also presents us with new decisions. We could wait and see what happens when we get there. But if we had the right tools, we could explore those potential decisions too. We could play out the "game" several steps ahead and mentally pre-experience the path to that goal. Our decision framework needs to include the likelihood of risk *consequences*, and the likelihood of *opportunities* presented by benefits. That will help us to see which choices matter most.

Changing Options

New decisions bring new opportunities to explore and new consequences to manage. If you want to reach a particular goal, you may have to carry out several decisions along the way. Each time you make one of those decisions, doors close and others open. You leave the territory you were in and move into a new realm. It's like moving from one Decision Island to another. Studying a map helps you navigate on heavily used paths. But you may be moving into uncharted territory where you need to make your own map. Looking ahead to expected decision points lets you chart likely options. Exploring your options will help prepare you for the decisions you expect to make. Having rehearsed your steps ahead of time will help you feel more at home in your new environment. That helps to build your confidence in a changing landscape.

Our decision framework should help us link new opportunities to events and new decisions. It should also help us map consequences to avoid, as we chart a path to our goal.

Making the Non-Decision

I'm sure you would agree that putting off a decision is not the same as making it. "Let's see how things play out," is a phrase we have all heard and perhaps have even spoken ourselves. When we use this to put off having to make a decision, are we really trying to let the decision be made for us? Are we not letting others decide the path we will have to take?

A stronger approach would be to "play out" the most likely scenarios in your mind and identify the options that you would most like. Then, even if you wait to "see how things play out," you will be tracking actual events against your mental pre-experience. You will be better prepared to act when the timing is right. You can recognize a situation instead of having it surprise you.

Not making a decision when you know you should is actually a decision: a decision to put off making a decision. You're making the "non-decision." You're ducking it. You are deciding to go forward without a decision, even though you would be better off with one. That's a bad decision, and is not the same as deciding that a decision made later would be better. If you don't have enough information to make a decision, you need to get that information. As long as you still have time to get it before you must make your decision, work on getting the missing information. Don't duck it because it takes a little more effort. Continue to work on making the decision. Perhaps after gathering more information you will be ready to make it. But when time is an issue for your decision, be ready for that decision-time. Prepare diligently, even though you may have to face some uncomfortable options. Work on deciding instead of just putting off your decision.

Fear is often the reason we duck when we see a responsibility-filled decision looming. Being able to pre-experience situations helps to build our confidence and address our fear. We also gain confidence from examining a track record of learning from our past decisions. Developing these skills will help give us courage to decide in favour of our desired future. Duck and it is no longer up to you. Make a decision in favour of your goals and step into *your* choice.

Secret Tip: **Don't duck a decision when you would be better off making one.**

Facing Dilemmas

Dilemmas happen when the risks, or their consequences, are significant for all your choices. No matter what you do, it seems like there is great risk. Sometimes, doing nothing also poses high risk. You don't want to face such a predicament alone. But before you involve others, you have an opportunity to consider which choice appeals to you the most. You may not be able to choose the option with the most benefit when facing a dilemma. Minimizing risk or negative consequences seems like a satisfying goal. See if there are any ways of minimizing those consequences, or at least preparing for them. Try to decide which of the consequences you would prefer to face, if it came to that.

Once you have identified your *own* preferences, you are better equipped to consider opinions of others. You need to ensure you trust and respect the people you involve. It may be tempting to tell everyone about your predicament, but it actually won't help you make a good decision. You may get some immediate sympathy for being in such a tight spot, but quandaries like this make for good gossip. Before you know it, your story may be a source of entertainment for your whole community. Resolving an impasse like this can be an emotionally draining experience. You don't need to take actions that add to your stress. Make choices that help you keep your emotional strength. Seek council from those who will respect your confidentiality. Perhaps even, talk to professionals who give guidance about dilemmas as part of their job.

These are difficult times, so make an effort to get enough sleep and eat for strength. Once you make the decision, you will need it to face the consequences. But you will not face them alone because you have involved people you trust. Turn to them. They will now support you.

Impossible Decisions

What makes a decision "impossible" is the huge emotional impact of the consequences. It can be a simple yes/no decision, a choice of several options, or even a dilemma. When the consequences carry overwhelming emotions, it seems impossible to make the decision. I hope you are never forced to make such a decision.

You grew up with a beloved pet that is now suffering with a serious illness. You hate to see them suffer, and the vet offers an option of relieving their pain permanently. This

can seem like an impossible decision. They can be much
worse.

Two aspects of impossible decisions can stop us. One is the
act of carrying out the decision, taking the action. The other
is the deciding part. We can sometimes ease the process by
asking someone else to act on the decision. We take no
action, ourselves. In cases of extreme emotion, we are also
tempted to ask someone else to decide for us. That can be a
mistake.

To help make the situation more manageable, separate the
decision into two parts. Understanding the best decision,
and applying it are not the same things. Use this to your
advantage. Try to get to the point where you can say that
you know what needs to be done, but you still can't do it.
Using logic and reason, look at the options and try to
identify the best choice. Get advice from experts. Try to rise
above your emotions for just long enough to understand the
options, risks and possible benefits. You can even try telling
yourself that you don't have to act on the decision (just yet);
you just have to understand what that would be. Come to
know the best decision.

Think about how you will see this decision in the far-distant future. Look back on this time from the future in your imagination. How would you feel then about having someone else make this important decision for you now? Would you see it as being their decision? Would you feel cheated out of making significant choices in your own life? Use your future perspective as a guide for what to do now.

Surround yourself with people you trust and who care about you. Draw emotional strength from them, family and friends. This is a time to pull together. They will be here for you. Use them for encouragement to do what you think is right. Explain to them the decision you have made. Tell them how you feel about the decision, and about acting on it. For grave decisions, the decision-maker may need to do some official act. Is that going to be you? If this is your decision, won't you want to be the one who makes it?

Chapter 3

Our Decision-Making Tools

We use tools to make our lives easier. We can achieve more things, faster and better when working with tools. So when it comes to decision making, what tools can we use to help us? Fortunately, we have both built-in tools, and methodologies that can work as powerful tools. We come fully equipped with logic, emotion, intuition and imagination. These are great tools to use with an appropriate method. To give them power, we can apply them with values, strategy and choice comparison techniques. Together, these tools can help to put us in control of our decisions.

Using Logic, Intuition and Emotion

Do we make decisions immediately through emotion, then use logic and reason to justify them? Desire and fear are two powerful emotions that drive our behaviour. As we explore in a later chapter, *Acknowledging Feelings*, our thinking-brain usually gets to process these low-level drives before we act. But if we let the impulses go through to action without thinking, then those in our environment control *us*. This is an old trick used by salespeople. Hook your emotions by dangling an object of desire (or warning of danger), then supply lots of reasons to justify the buy.

We have the brain circuitry to process these lower-level emotions, so we just need to use it to avoid living reactively. The thinking part of our brain can help us avoid attempts by others to manipulate us. It can also help us to identify goals and outcomes we desire. But getting there is the challenge. That is where the planning and logic parts of our brain come to our aid. Using those, we can see how to get to where we want to be. We can live proactively instead of reactively. *We* guide our lives, instead of letting the forces around us do it.

That sounds great, "Yes, I want to be in control of my life!" But beware of that "desire" emotion. It can compel you to make just that next decision in its favour. Fear can block you from choosing a benefit. Emotions are fond of directing our next decision. They seldom look ahead to see what the consequences will be, and they are not helpful for guiding us to long-term goals. For that, we need a path with a plan for actions. We design each action along the path to take us closer to our long-term goal. Then we know what we are doing, and why.

There is logic to that, and we can use logic to our advantage in preparing a plan. With logic, one thing depends upon another. Logic says, "If this happens, then we will be able to do that." That raises several question, such as, "How likely is 'this' to happen? What does it depend upon? What are our choices if it does not happen?" Knowing the answer to the second question probably helps you answer the first question. The last question is important for preparing a "Plan B." If you always have a "Plan B," you will feel more confident. If you don't have a "Plan B," you will feel more emotional about making your only plan succeed. That extra emotion could blind you to consequences and new opportunities.

Logic helps you to know what to do next and why. It helps you by identifying choices and addressing questions as you build a plan. The plan may not be perfect, but reviewing the plan can help improve it. Reviewing it with a person experienced in that subject area can improve it substantially. If not, it will increase your confidence in the plan, since you now have the opinion of a "subject matter expert."

Subject matter experts have a lot of experience with a particular subject area. They have seen it all, and been through it all. When they come upon a situation in their area that surprises them, they view it as an opportunity to learn something new. The fewer their surprises, the more of an expert they have become. When they come to a decision point in their procedures, they draw upon their vast experience to help them decide. Now they don't necessarily do that by using logic and the rules of "cause-and-effect." They could do that, but it can take a lot of time. Instead, they can rely on intuition to guide them.

A subject matter expert has extensive experience. They have an understanding of how things behave, and the underlying reasons why. They build mental models of how things work in their area of expertise. It is like a simulation in their mind. Ask them what will happen if some factor changes and they will know the answer faster than they can start to explain it to you. We call this *intuition*. Your experience is not the only source of intuition, but it is a good one.

You have the opportunity to become a subject matter expert on the topic that will affect your life the most: yourself. The more you pay attention to how you work, what you do and why, the more you will learn about yourself. If you try to make good decisions, you will learn what works and what doesn't. As time goes on, this build-up of expertise will give you a wealth of experience to draw upon. You will be able to make the best decisions for *you*, using your intuition. You will have a *feeling* about choices, and you will trust that feeling.

So we will build your *feeling* about a choice into our decision framework. We can add that to the structure we created for risks and benefits. This will help us to improve our perspective on decision choices.

Aligning with Values

Do you ever think about your values? What kind of principles do you value above others? Protecting little children from harm? Kindness? Do you even need to think about how important these values are to you? Other values you embrace may require more thought to recognize. People can decide what values they ascribe to and even sometimes rank them in order of importance. Then the most important ones might become a natural part of their behaviour. Perhaps a value of "being honest with myself" would be such a value. In another value, you might extend that honesty to others. Organizations can decide on values too, and even countries. Canadians, Australians and other Commonwealth citizens often value "peace, order, and good government." Americans sometimes ascribe to the Superman values of "truth, justice, and the American way."

Values are different from "rights" granted in a declaration or charter. The *Canadian Charter of Rights and Freedoms* (Government of Canada, 1982) grants "the right to life, liberty and security of the person." Unlike rights, values are principles that can provide guidance to us when we make decisions. To apply our values consistently in everything we do, we have to first recognize them and choose them as our guideposts.

If you rank your values, your top value should be one you always follow and never contradict, shouldn't it? Otherwise, isn't "having values" meaningless? Let's say you identify three values you want to live by and have ranked them in order. Can you say you have always stood by the top value? It's not always easy. At first, it takes thought. But then it becomes more natural. What about that third ranked value? It's still important, but maybe you are still striving to adhere to that value.

Once we start thinking about them, our values and their priority become clearer. Over time, we start applying them more automatically. Our established values can work for us in this way. We use them to guide us when we make a significant decision. We ask if a decision would be consistent with our values. Would we contradict any of our guiding values if we made a decision in a certain way? If so, perhaps we should consider a different choice.

Since values are important to the way we conduct our lives, we need to build them into our decision framework. We might be able to make a decision more easily if we knew how well each of its choices supported our values.

Play-acting with Imagination

One of your most powerful tools is your imagination. You used to use it all the time as a child. "Let's pretend..." is a phrase just loaded with possibilities. When you would say that, as a child, you were creating new situations with roles for your friends. You still have that ability to put yourself in a different role and see what it offers. The pretend role can give you new capabilities, skills, powers, authority and responsibilities. Your relationships are just descriptions, waiting to be enlivened.

When you were a child, you acted out these scenarios to see what happened. Now, you have greater mental abilities. You can act out scenarios in your mind, moving from one situation to another. How many steps ahead in a role can you take? As you start to feel the character's motivation, it becomes more natural to take another step. Look at this world through the eyes of this character. What are they likely to feel if you put them in a new situation? Can you pretend to feel that way, as them? What kind of decision are you likely to make, as them? Are you applying their motivation correctly?

These skills can be helpful to good decision-making. You can develop these skills further through improvisation and other forms of theatre. But even using your skills from childhood, you can imagine yourself in the future after making a certain choice. What does it feel like after acting on that decision? What new options open up to you? How are other people responding to your move? Have you gained more support, friends or enemies? What new decisions await you? Are you prepared to make them? This is an exploration of a particular direction. You're making decisions and choosing new options. You are imagining what it would be like to have taken those steps. You are exploring.

Another approach for using your imagination is to set your sights on a particular goal. You would like to see two things: what it would be like to achieve the goal, and the best way to get there. You can use logic to see which steps could take you in that direction. Mark out the major milestones for each path to that goal, since there may be more than one path. Now you are ready to use your imagination.

For the first path, what is the first decision you would have to make to get to the first milestone? Try making that decision in your imagination and moving from there towards the next milestone. How is it feeling? What is happening to the people around you? Is there a "gatekeeper" who won't let you proceed? What is their perspective? Try playing their role for a moment. Does that give you any ideas about how to deal with them? What should you do if you cannot get through a certain challenge successfully? Are you able to devise another path choice, such as a "Plan B?" Try this on the different paths you created with the milestones. Which path is your favourite, and why?

Once your imagination takes you through the milestones to reach your goal, live in it. Imagine what it is like, having come through that whole process and achieved your goal. What are your new challenges? Will you have the same friends? Will you be living in the same place? What will your life be like? Think about both the benefits and any new problems you may face.

How close is your imagination to reality? To get more of an idea, consider doing some research on a person who is already living the life you imagined. They are in the position you imagined, and followed their own path to get there. How similar is their path to the one you imagined for yourself? What is it like for them to be in that position? As you learn about the lives of people who have already achieved your goal, you can bring your imagination closer to reality. You may learn proven approaches from those who have overcome similar barriers to reach the goal. You can then adjust the plan for your path.

Exploring Strategy

Strategy harnesses your imagination to reach a goal. So, we can use strategy to help us tame our imagination for this mission. Instead of letting our imagination run wild, we give it the focus of our goal. Combining the power of imagination with the power of strategic focus gives us an amazing tool.

So what is strategy and how can we apply it? Using strategy is all about managing assumptions. Assumptions can be handy, especially when you acknowledge them and track them. If you plan to make a decision based on an assumption, it helps to remember the assumption. If you find the assumption to be false, you can revisit that decision and perhaps make another choice.

When we use assumptions about one thing causing another, we are using strategy. A strategy is a set of assumptions about cause and effect relationships. (Robert S. Kaplan, 1996, p. 30) The logic of our decisions is all about cause and effect relationships. A relationship may say, "If we do this (cause), then that will happen (effect)." If we want "that" to happen, we adopt a strategy of "we do this," so we can get "that" to happen.

Notice that something else could also cause it to happen. Several causes can sometimes bring the same result. If that is so, we couldn't prevent it from happening by adopting a strategy of "we don't do this." That strategy would only keep *us* from causing it to happen. Also, note that the assumption could be wrong in the first place. In that case, we have a "failed strategy." So it is important to examine the assumptions we use when working with a strategy to reach our goal. We don't want failed strategies.

Earlier, we looked at using our imagination to visualize a goal and the milestones along the path to get there. Identifying the milestones was straightforward. What we didn't discuss was what caused those milestone events to happen. If we wanted to make them happen, what could we do to cause them? We can come up with ideas like, "If we did this it might cause it to happen." That is an assumption about a cause and effect relationship. We're on the right track. If we think up some others like that, we can judge them and choose the most likely one.

In real life, likelihood and degree of certainty are often involved in the relationship. It is more like, "If we do this, and no one else interferes, then it is most likely that will happen to some degree." Life can be complicated. Nonetheless, building a strategy that helps us deal with situations is a great approach for success. We just need to remember our assumptions and their likelihoods.

For example, if my friends want me to go on a month-long trip with them next summer, I will need to save up for that. They explain how we will all travel and how much they expect it to cost each of us. I do some calculations and decide I need to save about one third of each paycheque from now until we leave. I call it my "save a third" strategy. If I save a third of my income from now until summer I can go on a great trip with my friends. My assumptions are that travelling will take this much money, over this number of weeks, including transportation, food and accommodation. Someone could drop out of the group, and then fewer of us would have to share the same costs. I would need more money. I need to remember my assumptions, in case the situation changes. Part way through, my "save a third" strategy might have to change to a "save half" strategy. Could I do it, or would I have to cancel my trip?

To help organize our strategy choices, we can use classic strategies for reference. A "fastest time" strategy would say, "If we always choose the quickest option, we will succeed sooner." An "easiest choice" strategy would say, "If we always take the easiest path, we will spend the least effort." The "righteous" strategy would say, "If we always choose what we know is right, we will be proud of our choices." The "efficient" strategy would say, "If we always choose the path of most gain for the least effort, we will make the most progress." The "hard work" strategy would say, "If we work hard, we will eventually reach our goal." The "influencer" strategy may say, "If I can get more people to like me, more people will do as I want."

So, false assumptions lead to failed strategies. Some of these strategies are valid, but none of them is likely to work in all situations. Proven strategies are those that have always worked in the past. They are a good bet, but they may not continue to repeat their past performance.

To create a useful strategy, we need to first clarify the goal. Then we need to assert good, supportable assumptions. Working at a high level gives us the most useful strategy. If you come up with several strategies, see if you can spot a commonality. Then try to create a strategy at a higher level that covers them all.

A good strategy serves as a guide to our decision making process. We have studied its assumptions and found them to be likely. We are confident that we will reach our goal if we follow this strategy. This gives us another tool, like values, to help guide us. Just as we use values to guide us when we make a significant decision, we can also use strategy. We ask if a decision choice would be consistent with our values. Now we can also ask if it would support our strategy. This adds more strength to our decision framework.

Secret Tip: **Strengthen your decision framework by knowing your values and strategy.**

Comparing Choices and Options

Earlier, we looked at pros and cons. This is a great way to start comparing choices. List each choice down the left column, and then create a column for pro factors and one more for cons. This works well for simple decisions. For decisions that are more complex, we need more detail. We can use the chart we made for risks and benefits. When facing several choices and other options, charting the decision might help.

Since we last considered the chart in *Figure 1* above, we have added several new factors to our decision framework. Let's create a new column for each of these options, as in *Figure 4*. For each risk, we can list consequences. For each benefit, we can list any opportunities. We can list likelihood for each of these in another column, on a 1 to 10 scale. It would be helpful if we could also capture our feelings about each choice. Sometimes, we know how we feel, but we can't express it well in words. We can use an enhanced scale to 10 for Feeling. Zero is for no feeling about it, and 10 is for feeling quite happy. For negative feelings, we can use a minus sign with the number. Minus one is for being a little uncomfortable. Minus ten is for total rejection.

Since high emotions can cloud our judgement, we want to recognize them. While you could register a big number for Feeling, showing either positive or negative emotion, we want to get beyond that. This number will be more helpful if you first become calm before thinking of it. Resist the temptation to register your anger, fear, jubilation or excitement through this number. You don't want those emotions informing your decision-making process. Calmly examine how you feel about this choice. We want your heartfelt attitude about the merits of choosing this option. "Happy" can still work for this, but in a calm way. "Sad," "disappointed" or "not good" might come to mind for a negative feeling. Try to get in touch with your true feeling instead of that raw emotion we can all feel.

When you list a choice for a decision, check the chart and see if the risks and benefits line up with your Feeling about the choice. If they don't, try to figure out why. Why don't you don't feel good about a choice with good benefits? Is it the high risk? Is there anything you can do to lower the risk? Can you prepare? Also, check whether you are feeling happy about a choice without good benefits. Are the risks low? Are you attracted to a low-risk option, even though it has little opportunity?

Let's add another column for your values. How consistent is each choice with your values? Here we can use the plus or minus 10 scale. A choice that fully supports your values would get a 10. If the choice does not relate to your values at all, give it a zero. If the choice goes directly against your values, give it a -10. So it is possible to have a choice with huge benefits that are quite likely, but is completely against your values. I'm guessing that choice might have some risks too. We see this in movies all the time. A casual attraction between two characters becomes an opportunity for an affair. The affair would bring fun, travel and expensive gifts. Cheating while in a committed relationship brings new risks. This plot line questions and challenges our characters' values. *Knowing* your values helps you make good choices.

If you are striving for a goal, how well does each choice support that goal? To find out, let's add another column with a plus or minus 10 scale for supporting your strategy. How well does each choice conform to your strategy? If it fully supports your strategy for reaching your goal, give it a 10. If it does not relate to your strategy, give it zero. If the choice undermines or harms your strategy to reach your goal, give it -10. Estimate a fitting number, if it is somewhere between the extremes.

For complex situations, we may need to address all these factors. It's good to know that we have them in case we feel the need to use them sometime. As *Figure 4* shows, we end up with 14 columns, including the name of the choice: **Choice**; **Risk**: Strength, Likelihood; **Consequence**, Likelihood; **Benefit**: Strength, Likelihood; **Opportunity**, Likelihood; *Feeling; Values Alignment; Strategy Support.* (The bolded headings are for labels, and the others are for numbers. The italicized headings apply to the whole choice, while the other numbers apply to the previous bold label.)

#	Choice	Risk					Benefit					Support for		
			Strength	Likelihood	Consequence	Likelihood		Strength	Likelihood	Opportunity	Likelihood	Feeling	Values	Strategy

Figure 4

Now we can do useful analysis for this decision. For each choice, we can say to what degree it is consistent with your values. How well it supports your strategy. How you feel about it. How risky it is, what those risks are, how likely they are and what their likely consequences would be. How big the benefits of each choice would be and how likely they are. What opportunities are likely to come with each benefit? Looking at the chart reveals the answers to all these questions. You have captured it and don't have to rely on just your memory any more. You can also explain it to other people much more easily than when it was only in your mind.

Most decisions are not complex enough to justify exploring all the consequences and opportunities. Still, you might want to take Feeling, Value Consistency and Strategy Support into account. We can use a smaller version of the chart for those situations, shown in *Figure 5*.

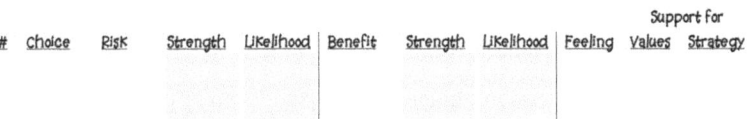

#	Choice	Risk	Strength	Likelihood	Benefit	Strength	Likelihood	Feeling	Support for Values	Strategy

Figure 5

Decision Shortcuts

When you are thinking about a choice, you might find a shortcut by considering the last three factors first. They are Feeling and support for Values and Strategy. For convenience, we can refer to these as *Foundation Factors*. If any of these factors have negative numbers, what possible benefit would make you choose this option? Have you heard any stories of a good decision where the person said, "I felt great misgivings about it and I didn't think it was right, but I did it anyway and it turned out to be the best thing ever!" Maybe for a rollercoaster ride, but even there it is doubtful. If you have a bad feeling about a choice, why choose it? If you must explore it further, analyse it well.

If you don't feel good about a choice, it could also be due to its lack of consistency with your values. If you make significant decisions that support your values, you will feel better about your life. When you are trying to reach a goal, and have devised a strategy to reach it, focus on that. Significant decision choices that provide no support for your strategy should not distract you. Try to stay focused on the path to your goal.

Look at these three Foundation Factors first: Feeling and

support for Values and Strategy. If any of them have low or negative numbers, you need to have a good reason to estimate risk and benefit. We can often skip considering choices that fail this initial test. In the *Incentives and Threats* section below, we explore this concept a little further. Also, check that your number for Feeling comes from a calm place. If you are quite emotional about this choice, your Feeling number will be distorted by that anger, fear, excitement or desire. Try to register your Feeling number when you can be calm about it. By starting with a look at your Foundation Factors, you could quickly eliminate this choice, or justify further examination.

Secret Tip: **Consider discarding choices that don't feel right or support your values or strategy.**

A Visual Approach

Since we have added new factors to our decision framework, we should also portray them visually. This will make it easier for many people to relate to your choice options. Let's look at a more complex situation where a graphical approach might help us grasp it more quickly.

Terrence wants to get a bike to ride to school and work, and to use for fun on weekends. He has shopped around local stores and tried out a few bikes. The high-end bikes really appeal to him, with their light carbon frames and responsive handling. Unfortunately, they cost several times his available budget. He would have to borrow most of the money for a high-end bike. The bikes at the lower end of the price list are within his budget. They are heavier and handle a little more sluggishly, but they would be better than not having a bike.

Another option is to buy a used bike through an online ad. There he might be able to find a higher-end bike that he could afford. If he buys through a certain store he likes, he can use their scan and motion-capture bike fitting system as part of the deal. He is not a bike expert and is a little skeptical about buying a used bike from a stranger. To see his choices more clearly, Terrence used the decision framework to record his numbers. He found that he didn't see any opportunity differences between his choices, so he left that part out. *Figure 6* shows his assessment, which we discuss in more detail.

#	Choice	Risk	Strength	Likelihood	Consequence	Likelihood	Benefit	Strength	Likelihood	Feeling	Support for Values	Strategy
1	High end	Borrow $	8	10	Lose Bike	6	Easy ride	7	10	6	8	8
2	Low end	Unhappy	5	4	Won't ride	4	Fit System Afford it	7 8	9 10	7	9	9
3	Used	Worn out	7	6	Repair $$	7	Afford it	8	10	5	7	8

Figure 6

While the high-end bike is so attractive, Terrence is not sure he can afford it even with a loan. The payments would be large. Since his job is temporary, he wonders about his ability to pay back any loan over time. If he could not make the payments in the future, he would lose his bike. It is a great ride, but he has mixed feelings about it.

If he gets a bike that isn't as much fun for him, he worries that he may not ride it on weekends. A lower priced bike would be fine to get him to school and work, and he wouldn't feel the burden of payments. It fits his values and supports his need for transportation. He could also help ensure a good match by using the store's bike fitting system. The store is currently promoting it by including a fit with certain lower priced bikes.

He could get a *used* high-end bike, but he doesn't feel confident about knowing that it would not need repairs soon. He is not very familiar with high-end bikes and would have to find a way not to pay more than the used bike is worth. Not one of his friends has a high-end bike. His goal is to get a bike he can use mainly for transportation, so the high-end part would just be for fun. A used bike might be a workable solution, but he is still unsure.

Let's see how his ratings from *Figure 6* look for the used high-end bike choice, when we diagram them, as shown in *Figure 7.*

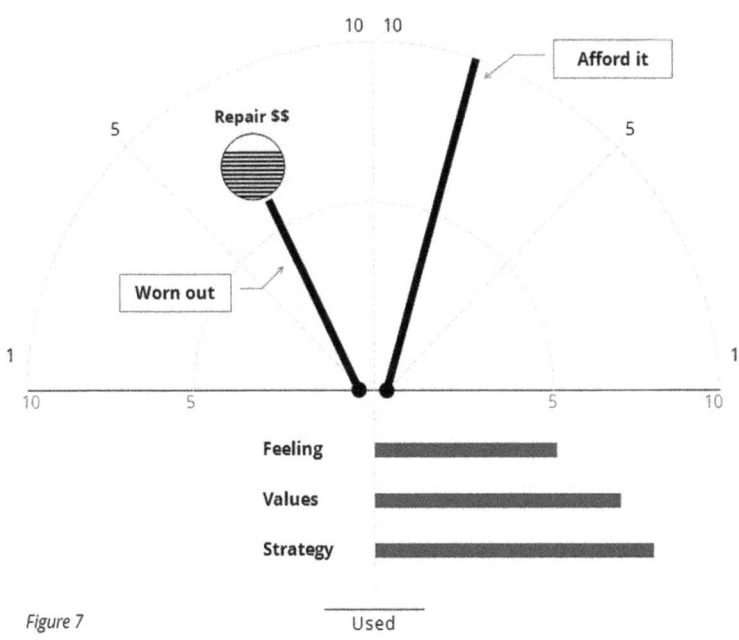

Figure 7

Interpreting the Diagrams

Figure 7 shows a certain (definite) benefit, which is that Terrence can afford the used bike. But the risk is likely that he will get stuck with repair costs if the bike is worn out. We see the consequence of Repair $$ shown as a circle at the end of the "Risk" line, filled to seven with its degree of Likelihood.

The Foundation Factors are at the bottom of the choice lines. They expand sideways from the middle to show positive ratings to the right, and negative ratings to the left. Even though the used bike choice does support his strategy, and his values to some degree, he doesn't feel strongly about it. The top horizontal line clearly shows his mild feeling of five, extending only halfway.

The above diagram in *Figure 7* gives us a visual way to grasp Terrence's take on the Used Bike option. When we chart all of his ratings together, it becomes easier for us to compare the choices visually. *Figure 7a* does this for us.

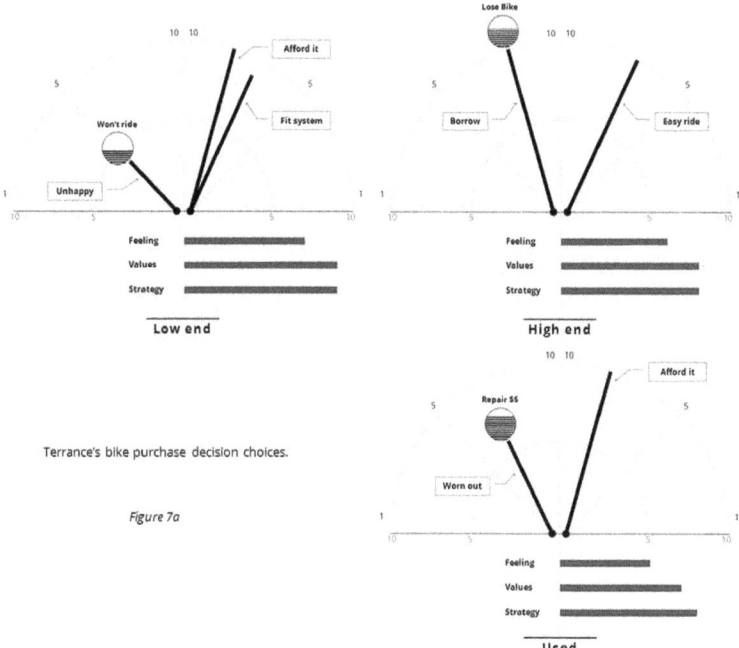

Terrance's bike purchase decision choices.

Figure 7a

We can visually compare the "High end" diagram in *Figure 7a* with the "Used" bike diagram below it. The "High end" chart clearly shows more risk and less benefit, even though he has stronger Feeling for it. The "Low end" choice has the least risk with the most benefit. It is the most conservative and least stressful choice. Seeing the charts of all the choices together helps us analyse the options more quickly. We often call this kind of display a "dashboard," since it lets you see the information you have gathered, all at once. Let's analyse what our dashboard is showing us.

Terrence's "High end" choice shows a risk angle of eight and a benefit of seven. The combined angle is 15 units out of a possible 20. This choice is somewhat stressful, but since both are certainties, he knows what to expect. Still, it is not attractive. The one consequence of the risk shows a good likelihood to lose the bike if he cannot make loan payments. That stress is all for an "easy ride" benefit. Terrence would say that it is a "beautiful" ride, since he took one of those bikes for a test ride at the store. It is impressive and Terrence is emotional about it, but his feelings are a little mixed. Let's look at those in more detail.

Terrence's desire for a high-end bike shows in his Feeling score on this high-end choice. While excited, he is also feeling uncomfortable with such a big purchase price. It is far beyond what he can afford, or needs to spend. So he gave it a Feeling of six. He rated the consistency with his Values as eight because having this kind of bike would last him a lifetime. It would be an investment in his future, perhaps. That's what he told himself. He gave an eight rating as support for his Strategy because the high-end bike would get him to school and work in fine style.

As you can see by the Foundation Factors in *Figure 7a*,

Terrence didn't feel as strongly about the used bike choice. But buying a new lower-end bike did feel right to him. It also was much more consistent with his Values, since he would not have to carry any debt for it. He gave his Strategy support a higher rating for this choice than he did the others. He wanted a new bike that would be trouble-free and well suited to him. Given that the store promotion included the fitting system, this choice was better suited to his goal.

For Terrence's "High end" choice, risk is more vertical and therefore stronger. Likelihoods are both certain. The other two choices have stronger benefits than risk. The likelihoods of their risk are less than the "High end," as well. The best-looking choice is for the low-end bike, showing an added benefit of the fit system with a strong likelihood. Even if Terrence is unhappy with this bike and wishes he were riding a high-end bike, the likelihood of that risk's consequence is low.

Terrence listed the consequences in his decision framework table for each of the choices. We see these as circles at the end of the "Risk" lines, each filled with their degree of Likelihood. For example, the "won't ride" consequence circle is at the end of the "Unhappy" risk line in the "Low-end" case. We see it filled up not even halfway with likelihood, since Terrence rated its likelihood at a four. Terrence chose to buy the lower-end bike.

As we learned earlier, Terrence did not see special opportunities coming from any of the benefits. For the sake of discussion, let's pretend that the fitting system he saw at the store fascinated him. It appealed to him so much that he wondered if he could master it and perhaps get a job using it for customers at the store. If he bought a bike from the store, and learned all he could about the system, he might improve his chances of getting that job. How should we show that potential opportunity in relation to the Fit System benefit? *Figure 8* shows the New Job opportunity at the end of the Fit System benefit line.

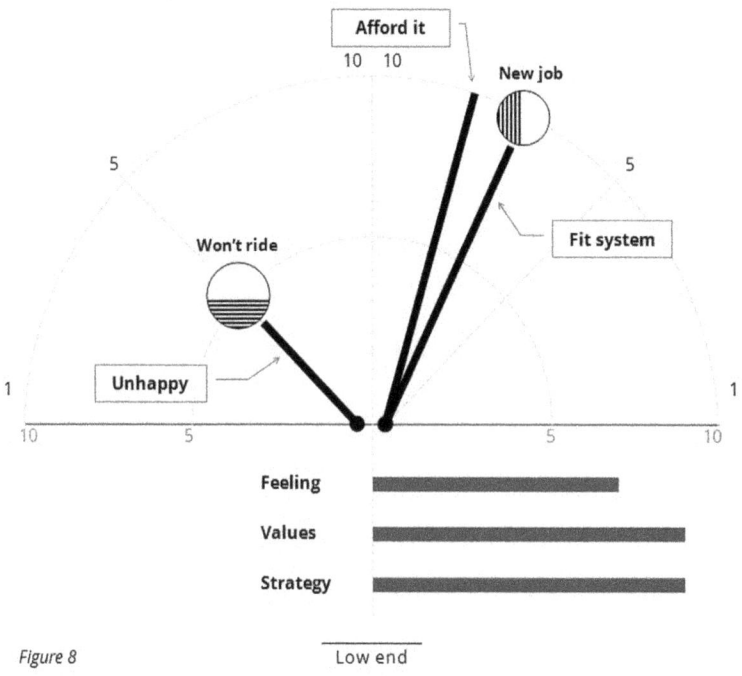

Figure 8

We rate the likelihood of the New Job opportunity happening at only four. If Terrence were to study it first and present himself as quite knowledgeable about it, we would raise that number. We show likelihoods for opportunities as fills of the circle, expanding from left to right. This way, we easily see them as different from the circles of consequences.

Showing Cost

We did not show cost in the diagrams for Terrence's decision. If we had, it would display as an almost horizontal risk line, with a full extension for likelihood. Since we know the cost in this case, it is certain and represents little or no risk. For Terrence, the cost of the bike would be at least the same for all three choices. He had set aside a certain amount that he wanted to spend on the bike and he wanted to get the best bike he could for that money. He would spend that amount in any of the three choices. For the high-end bike, he would have to borrow money and spend more, but he would also spend the amount he had set aside. So the borrowed money shows as extra risk.

We show cost as a risk of full certainty, since we usually know the amount. The angle, or strength, of the risk depends on the impact that spending will have on you. Since Terrence had already set aside that amount of money for the bike, spending it would not impact him much at all. The angle of that risk line would be small. Because the risk was small and the same in all three choices, we did not show it in this example. We also wanted to introduce the diagram concept without extra clutter. If you wanted to be completely accurate, you could include the cost in the diagrams and the number chart. Usually, we leave out ratings that do not influence any of the choices.

Secret Tip: **Diagram your choices to get a**
visual impression.

Drawing the Diagrams

You can draw the diagrams as a sketch, a scale drawing, or imagined in your mind. After you have drawn a few, as either a sketch or a scale drawing, it becomes easier to draw them in your imagination. You might even skip the step of picking and recording numbers. You could visualize the diagram angles and line lengths directly from your knowledge of the situation. But drawing them can be fun, and it allows you to share them with others.

Understanding Strength and Likelihood

Imagine a stressful choice with a risk and benefit of ten units each. Lines for each would go straight up. Now extend them both almost fully for Likelihood. This *would* be a stressful choice. The risk is huge and almost certain. But the benefit is also huge and almost certain. This kind of choice with such a big risk should have a benefit that contributes to your personal growth or development. That might make it a more attractive choice, even though both likelihoods are high.

You may come across some unusual combinations of risk and benefit that have opposite likelihoods. We see two extreme examples of risk and benefit in *Figure 9*.

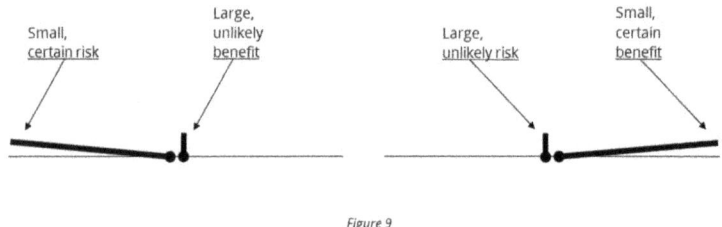

Figure 9

In each case, we see lines of drastically different lengths. On the left side we see a small but certain risk, like a payment, along with a large benefit. While the benefit is potentially quite large, it is unlikely. An example of this choice could be buying a lottery ticket.

On the right side, we see a very large risk that is unlikely, along with a small but certain benefit. An example of this could be a dare to do something risky and unfamiliar. The benefit is to preserve your pride. The dare could be to dive off the high platform into a pool for the first time. It is unlikely you will be injured, but if you are it could change your life.

In these cases, we are seeing that both risk and benefit use a unit of one on the diagram. (For real life situations, the number may be only a fraction of one.) On the left, we have one unit of certain risk strength with one unit of benefit likelihood. On the right, we have one unit of risk likelihood with one unit of certain benefit strength. We have nicknamed these types of choices "Happy Landings" and "Risky Takeoffs," inspired by their appearance. Happy Landings are "Low-risk" choices with a sketchy benefit. Risky Takeoffs are "mainly-Risk" choices because there is so little benefit, and a chance of disaster.

Happy Landings can be fun, as long as you won't feel too disappointed if it doesn't work out. Risky Takeoffs are choices of daredevils, or of friends you might call foolish or stupid. Another example of a Risky Takeoff choice is getting a ride home with a drinking driver. If you are lucky, you may get home safely, but it will be a tragedy otherwise. Both types of choices involve chance, but with very different stakes. If you beat the odds with a Happy Landings choice, things are great. Risking the odds in a Risky Takeoff choice can be the worst day of your life.

Keep a lookout for those large, unlikely risks. Think them over carefully. For Risky Takeoff choices, the unlikely risk is much larger than the certain benefit. Remember that the **strength** of a risk or a benefit is far more significant than its likelihood. A low likelihood (short line) says that chances are slim that it will happen. Applying that to a strong risk or benefit (large angle) means something **big** really could happen! There is a chance, even though it may be little.

Using New Perspective

Working with these diagrams can help us look at our decision choices more logically. We can talk about the diagrams as we share our opinions about choices with others. Yet, it is important to remember that we base these diagrams on the numbers of initial guesses. We wanted to get an idea of how we view the situation we are facing. Once we look deeper into the facts and gain more knowledge of the situation, we may see things differently.

The ancient Greek philosopher Plato said, "A good decision is based on knowledge and not on numbers." So it is critical that we find ways to get good quality information before we choose a plan of action. Once we have gained the knowledge we need, we can use charts and diagrams to digest and communicate realistic options. Which of our strengths and likelihoods are initial guesses? Which ones have we verified with other sources? You could use colour in your charts, like red numbers to show initial guesses. Green numbers could show agreement among sources or advisors. We'll explore this idea more in a moment.

The original idea of recording our view of choices as numbers was a way for us to involve the thinking part of our mind. Now we have a technique we can use to go beyond just feeling the situation we face. We can use our mind to describe our choices and show them to others. We can then recognize areas where we need to know more, especially if we use colour. We can develop questions and look for specific answers. We can bring those answers back to a familiar framework where we replace initial guesses with knowledge. We can make an informed decision. As we make more of those, we become more comfortable with our process. We look for missing information to fit into our framework. Our informed decisions become more of a way of life for us. As a result, our decisions become better. We focus on making good decisions.

Chapter 4

Gathering Useful Information

Lack of information is one of the greatest challenges to making good decisions. You can use assumptions to imagine choice consequences or opportunities. But you must remember the assumptions on which you based those projections. The quality of your final decision will depend on the quality of your information. Yes, you can still make a bad decision with good information. But you are most likely to make a bad decision if you have wrong information.

Basing a decision on wrong information undermines your confidence for future decisions. Anger creeps in and eventually becomes self-directed. Regardless of where you got the information, you tend to blame yourself for not confirming it. This is something from which you must recover. Like an injury, we should avoid needing recovery. Let's try to ensure accurate information for our decisions.

Prefer trusted sources. Rate critical information you gather, using a scale for "degree of confidence." Perhaps a scale up to 10 would suffice. Alternatively, you can use colour as previously mentioned. You could use a degree of confidence scale going from red (guesses) through orange (rumour) and yellow (pretty sure) to blue-green (verified). You can either use the numeric or colour scale when discussing your decision, and when deciding. Use an unrelated source to confirm important information and increase your degree of confidence in it. If you can't confirm it, lower your degree of confidence. For the numeric scale, if you are starting with hearsay or a rumour, give it a zero degree of confidence. If you are imagining possibilities and guessing, give that a negative degree of confidence. You can still use it to explore your options, but good decisions need a high degree of confidence.

To communicate visually, you can use the degree of confidence colour to help understand the status of strengths and likelihoods. The colour codes can also help you with Foundation Factors while you are still working on them. This helps to make the information you already have more useful.

Thinking about Questions

The best way to get good information is to ask good questions. So how do you come up with good questions that are relevant to your decision outcomes? Sometimes, obvious questions seem to present themselves, but can be distractions. The farther you go down the path they suggest, the farther away you get from your decision model. You are not investigating a crime, here. You are trying to get accurate information about choices, risks, consequences, benefits and opportunities.

Sometimes, an obvious question suggests an even better question. For example, let's say that a friend of yours is trying to decide whether to buy an expensive item. They would like you to help them think through their options. The obvious question is, "How much does it cost?" The next is, "Wow, do you have that much?" If you keep going down this path though, focus is likely to remain on dealing with the purchase price. You might ask that last question as, "Wow, can you afford it?" This is a better question because it could also refer to ongoing costs. In the context of the conversation though, the interpretation will likely be, "Can you pay the purchase price?"

Total "affordability" is the real issue. Once your friend has made the purchase, there may be other costs that just keep going. They might have to get a "thing" for it. Other issues could include monthly or annual costs. There may be costs for supplies, storage fees, security measures, service fees, maintenance, loan payments, insurance, or perhaps licensing fees. Ongoing costs can add up to an unpleasant shock down the road. Anticipating future costs comes from imagining living with the new item. Imagine dealing with both the benefits and the costs on a daily basis. The "total cost of ownership" starts to become clear and new questions arise. Try to pose questions around the issues of risk and consequences. Come at it from a broad perspective, at first.

To get a fuller picture, also ask your friend questions about expected benefits and opportunities. Try a couple of different "roles," like being excited and skeptical. It's great that they can now take advantage of new opportunities because of this purchase. That's exciting. You are sure that they will for the first week or two, at least. Will they continue after three months? You know your friend. Are they likely to continue benefiting from this purchase over the course of a year? Divide the cost by the number of months you think your friend will use it. That is the cost per useful month. Is it worth it? The ongoing costs continue after that. Have you ever known anyone with a gym membership that they didn't use regularly? The benefit is available, but you don't get it if you don't use it.

You are your own best friend. At least, you should strive to be. When we face decisions ourselves, we can tend to focus on emotional questions. Thinking of your decision as your friend's decision could help. It could give you the emotional distance you need to ask good questions. Focus your questions on risk and consequences. Play the roles of living after the decision. Pose questions about pursuing the opportunities, and enjoying the benefits. Don't try to answer them yet. Just try to come up with relevant questions. You can fill in answers later on.

Secret Tip: **Ask yourself questions about your decision as if it were your friend's.**

Facts and Assumptions

It's human nature to use assumptions for facts. If we don't know an answer, we assume one or guess. That's not a problem as long as we acknowledge that we are exploring an assumption. When we face a decision, we need verified facts. We can explore options based on assumptions repeatedly, but we want to base our decision on researched facts. Having a list of relevant questions brings structure to our quest for facts. When you have accurate answers to the questions about risks and benefits of a choice, you are ready to start making your decision. You can compare choices and options with known confidence in your information.

The problem with assumptions is that some of them are attractive to us. We can attach to them emotionally or intellectually. During our research, we must then try to replace that assumption with a researched fact. What happens to our emotional investment when the researched fact does not agree with our assumption? We experience disappointment, or even worse, denial. Isn't it better to feel happy about a *fact* than an *assumption*? To achieve that, we can try to reserve our judgment about assumptions. We can view them as just possibilities to explore. We can try to save our emotional investment for options we have explored more fully, and found to be credible. It is the difference between happiness based on hope or certainty. One feels higher, and one feels deeper.

Negative assumptions can be even more of a problem. They

are dangerous when they move from being "may not" to being "won't." If your assumption is that something "may not" work, you are somewhat detached and still reserving some judgment. It is not as detached as "we don't know, but we'll see," but is still not too emotional. When your assumption is something "won't" work or happen, it is likely to block any further exploration. Here you are. You don't know. You have not looked into it. You have not asked any questions. You have not found any answers. Yet, you say it "won't" work or happen, and you will not explore it any further. That is an emotional attachment to a negative assumption. Why would you take that position? It could be fear, desire, or any of the usual culprits. It contributes to ignorance.

It's not that you can't or shouldn't use assumptions. They can be quite useful in exploring options and conducting "what if" scenarios, as long as you stay detached. When one of those scenarios is so attractive, or so scary, that we believe it emotionally, we cannot make a good decision.

The facts we seek do not protect us from emotion. But we usually do not know all the facts. Facts carry with them contributing factors. This make them more complicated. "He was found guilty." You can know the resulting fact from all the contributing factors, and still not know all the factors. Some of them may be important to you and your decision. Facts are not necessarily simple. So you may need to add a "degree of certainty" to the facts you find. The more you look into it, the more certain you may become that you see this fact in this way. In the end, you will base decisions on the way *you* see things.

Anticipating Events

Can you predict what someone else will do? The likelihood of you being successful at that depends somewhat on how well you know them. If you know them quite well, you are much more likely to predict what they will try to do in a given situation. They may fail at their attempt. You can try to predict their successfulness, too. That may depend on others who are also involved. It can get complicated.

Instead of predicting the outcome of an event, can you determine the three most likely outcomes? That sounds a lot easier, doesn't it? For most of your decisions, that is your primary research goal. "The outcome will either be this, that, or that other thing." It's a great place to start, and it's doable.

Out of those three things, which is the least likely to happen? If you can't tell, look into the situation some more until you can. Of the two remaining possible outcomes, which one do you think is more likely? How sure are you that it will happen, on a scale of 1 to 10? That's your likelihood for that outcome. You are less sure that the second choice will happen. How sure are you on the second choice, and the third, on the 1 to 10 scale? If you feel like you are making wild guesses here, look into the situation some more. After becoming more familiar with it, revise your rating numbers. If you are using confidence colours, revise them too.

Try this out on familiar things that don't matter much, just for practice. Which one of three possible things is most likely to happen tomorrow morning at your house? What likelihood rating do you give each of the three? Which one happened? What was your likelihood rating for that? Increase your challenge to some other familiar situation, such as school or work. Pick three possible things that are most likely to happen there. Rate their likelihoods. Which one happened? What was your likelihood rating for it? This can be fun if the things that happen do not affect you at all.

Increase your challenge to things that will affect you, but

only slightly. It could be as simple as which of three friends will you see first tomorrow? What are your likelihood ratings? Now, decide the first thing you are going to say to each one. Which friend was it? What was your likelihood rating on that? Did you follow through and say the planned thing to them? As an exercise, think up another future situation that will involve you making a simple decision. Make your choices and rate them. Decide ahead of time what to do or say for each of the three choices. Try it out. Do things go as planned, or were there surprises?

How are these exercises like making important decisions? Even though you plan gentle exercises, you live through the challenges of preparing for outcomes. Then, the choices you prepared for may not be the only ones presented. If that happens to you, you will soon realize that you also need to prepare for the unexpected. You may need to expand your anticipated choices beyond the three you have been imagining. You may also find that your "degree of confidence" accuracy improves for the most likely outcome. Practice brings experience. Experience is a great educator.

Secret Tip: **Plan for what you expect, but also prepare yourself for the unexpected.**

Opinions of Others

The way you see things is unique. Your experiences and your history give you a reference point from which to view situations and events. You automatically compare everything new that you experience or imagine to what you know. So does everyone else. That's why they see things differently sometimes. It can be hard to put ourselves in their position and see things their way without talking to them. When we do, we get a whole new vista.

Even though we may agree on things, we each view situations from our own perspective. The more varied our backgrounds are, the more we can learn from each other. Learning about how someone else sees a situation can help us find choices that we didn't see before. If they have already dealt with a similar situation, we might learn from their experience. If they are an expert in these situations, they can give us specialized guidance. Seek their wisdom.

Asking and Listening

People will give you different information depending on what *they* think you need to know. So unless you are asking a formal question, like when using a microphone, tell people why you want their advice or opinion. This will give them a framework for their response. If this person is new to you, have a short conversation and explain your need for perspective on your topic. Tell them about the decision you are considering and why you need more information. Ask them if they now see why you came to them and want their opinion. Be sure they know what you would like from them. Then listen. Even though you have set up a conversation, keep your response to head nods and one or two syllable words. Let them talk. Let them keep talking. You have created a special time and space here that you likely won't experience with them again. Soak it in. Questions may arise in your mind. Do not interrupt this person with them. Take note of your questions, to ask them later. It's okay to acknowledge that you understand as you go along, or say so if you don't understand. If they have any real need for more information or clarity from you, they will ask you for an explanation. Give it completely, but briefly. Value their time and be respectful of it.

After they have shared their viewpoint and offered advice, be sure to thank them. The conversation will then likely become more casual. This is a good time to ask any questions that you noted while they were speaking. Also, ask any remaining question that you prepared before the meeting. Feel free to interact with them in a more natural way, now that they have expressed their point of view.

Why conduct the interview this way? To ensure you receive their viewpoint. You selected this person for their experience, position, ability and expertise. You want to hear what they have to say. When we converse with people, we interrupt their thought process. We change the course of the conversation by introducing our own thoughts along the way. The other person responds to what you just said, instead of speaking about the thoughts they were forming. Those thoughts could have been important to you, but you may never know. The conversation may never get back to a point that reminds the other person about them.

If you are in a casual conversation, it is normal for the topic to wander. Even when the subject becomes more serious, a conversation with a friend is casual in its structure. You always talk to each other, so if they leave anything unsaid, they will bring it up in the future. That's the luxury of conversations with friends and family. They continue to happen.

Managing Crowd Pressure

You see them all the time. Every day you talk with the same people. You may "text" with them at all hours. They ask you questions about yourself. They give you their opinion on things you are facing. They form a force you can feel. How long could you resist if they all wanted you to do something? Having not one person who agrees with you weakens your resolve.

We bend to the pressure exerted by our friends and family. They are our community and we share our life with them. If you feel that your purpose in life is to support their decisions and conduct your life as *they* see fit, then do as they say. If you prefer to choose your own path to the goals that you set, then you will need to manage this force around you.

Once you make a decision, people around you are facing a new reality. They adjust to that, whether they were for it or against it. Their attitude towards you may change, until you resolve the feelings between you. That resolution effort is a consequence of your decision, so you can plan for it.

Let's say you are about to make an important decision. It will mean you will not be able to see your friends and family as often as you do normally. It might involve travel. If you decide to do it though, you will likely benefit. This can be a hard decision to make, especially if none of your friends wants to give up being with you. Keeping your decision from them until you make it is not an option. They can tell that you are considering something big. You could try to wait to tell them about it until after you decide, but they will pry. If you deny or resist, they will unite and all focus on just this topic.

You have two issues: the decision itself, and how best to handle your family and friends. If you had finished making the decision, you could just tell them all about it and they would deal with it. You might have to smooth the way with some of them, but eventually they would accept your decision. Right now though, you are not yet ready to make your decision. Do you involve them?

At least one of the choices for your decision does affect your friends and family, since they will not be able to see you often. They will not like that. If you have a broad range of relationships in your circle, their positions could fall into one of three categories. First, they understand the benefit you seek and will support whatever decision you make. Even though they will miss being with you, they just want the best for you. Second, you cannot possibly consider pursuing this because it will ruin your life. You will regret it, and they threaten never to speak to you again if you do it. Third, you should definitely go for it, and forget what everyone else says since it is your life.

Since the decision affects them, it seems fair to tell them ahead of making it final. The question is, are you telling them to help manage their acceptance of the outcome, or do you want their input? The second group above is the most difficult to deal with in both cases. They feel threatened by anything that disrupts your relationship. It is all about them. If you have people like them in your circle, you will have to plan an approach to calm them down. The first and third groups need little or no help in accepting any decision you make.

You will get opinions and advice from all three groups. The first group might include people who can offer useful experience to help inform your decision. The second and third groups should not influence your decision, since they are personally biased. The second group worries about the pain they will suffer. The third group is imposing its attitude towards most things in life, onto your decision. They are telling you how they would decide and advising you to do what they would do. They are not considering your situation as you see it.

The benefit of telling your circle of friends and family about your upcoming decision is twofold. You have more time to manage their reactions, and there may be some people in the first group who could enrich your perspective. The risk of telling them ahead of making your decision final is that you may not be able to ignore the urging of people in groups two and three. They may influence your final decision. Since they are on opposite sides of the issue and quite vocal, they will add a lot of noise to any conversations within your circle. Their disagreement may increase emotional tension and this will somehow become your fault. Then it will be your problem to deal with. High frustration likes to shoot blame.

A possible solution you may be thinking about is to tell just those in the first group who could help you. Let's call them the alpha sub-group. If you brought them into your "inner-circle" they would have to keep your deciding process a secret until you were ready to announce your decision. You would have to get enough assurance from them to be successful in hiding this process from all the others. If the others detected that you were in a quandary, they would pry and pressure you for answers. Once you announce your decision, do you reveal the members of your alpha sub-group? This would show that you have been keeping secrets from the others for privacy reasons. How is privacy valued in your circle? Would it be okay with them if you sought council from just these few? If not, are you asking members of the alpha sub-group never to reveal their prior knowledge?

If you decide on using this approach, how do you determine the best members of your alpha sub-group? We know that they must be able to keep your situation confidential, even though they know many others in your circle. As we mentioned above in *Opinions of Others*, we want those who have faced a similar situation before, so we might learn from their experience. If they are an expert or a professional in these situations, they may even give specialized guidance. You may have to do some research on your candidates, to see if they have dealt with a similar situation in their past. You could express an interest in getting to know more about them. Be sure to get their agreement of confidentiality before telling them about your upcoming decision.

It can be tricky to invite people to your "Decision Island."

They want to know what is to be kept confidential and for how long. They will feel better about it if they can talk with others on your Island. Tell them that you need their advice on something, but it needs to remain confidential. Ask them if they agree not to tell anyone about it until you make a decision. Tell them how long you think that might take. If they agree, tell them about any others who also know. Tell them if it is okay for them to talk together, as long as they keep it to themselves. Tell this person that you are trusting them. Then tell them why you need their advice.

You are asking a big favour of these people in your inner-circle. You want them to keep your secret until you make a decision. You also want the benefit of their experience. This should not be a drawn-out process. Prepare for this time by understanding your own position and creating your questions for them. Be ready to get everyone "on board" as close to the same time as possible. Get their advice and be ready to decide. Keep the time on your "Decision Island" as short as possible. Decide and then get out. Reveal your decision to everyone. Your "Decision Island" has served its purpose.

Secret Tip: **Try to decide quickly once you have asked other people to keep your confidence.**

Dealing with Authority Forces

We grow up with authority all around us. It tells us about rules of behaviour and enforces them. As little kids, we feel we have no choice but to follow authority. Often, it is to protect us. We try to avoid the consequences of not complying. Over time, we start to understand why other people are concerned about what we do. Our behaviour affects them to some degree. So authority forces are set up as a limiting factor to guide our behaviour. In the best cases, they also encourage us.

Parental and school authority can be frustrating at times. If you are facing that now, there are two keys to dealing with it. The first is to recognize the role that authority is playing in your decision-making model. It factors in a big way with consequences. The risks of not complying with the limits set by parents and school can be huge. So, instead of focusing on those limits, consider pushing limits of your ability. Consider challenging yourself to become excellent in something. You could choose something at which you are already good, or something new. Choose something acceptable to, and not affected by limits of authority. Why? So you can develop expertise. Your decisions will still be challenging, but you can get help with them from more sources. By developing expertise, you will learn a valuable approach that you can always apply in the future. If you ever need to develop expertise again, you will know what to expect and how to go about it. That skill will change your life.

The second key to dealing with parental and school authority is to recognize that it is temporary. Even though you should comply at this time, make a note about the choice you would have made if you were not subject to their authority. In time, you will be of an age when you are beyond their authority. At that point, review the choice in question. See if you still would like to act on the choice you preferred at that time. If so, now is your chance for a new decision. Consider it and act accordingly. If your review of the past gives you fresh understanding of that situation, you can use it as experience. Perhaps a path not taken, thank goodness. It is important to learn from our experiences and the choices we made.

In general, authority forces are always willing to provide advice on choices. You can count on them for an opinion. Since they are so reliable, it may be a good idea to check in with them for their perspective on your decision. You can rate their opinion along with any others you get. They are usually clear about risks and consequences, making sure you haven't overlooked any. But sometimes they can be a little light on benefits and opportunities. If your situation does not fall within their area of expertise, they will tell you. They may also refer you to an expert if you want to follow up with one. They will expect you to follow their advice, and they may want to track your decision now that they know about it. It doesn't mean you have to follow their advice, but they will want to check for any rule violations.

Initially, authority forces are there to guide us. They even sometimes make decisions for us. Eventually, we take responsibility for our own decisions. We become our own authority. We work with other authority forces to negotiate our way through life. We find solutions to common problems and create new entities. We empower ourselves, and those around us.

Chapter 5

Projecting Decision Outcomes

"Decide in your heart of hearts what really excites and challenges you, and start moving your life in that direction. Every decision you make, from what you eat to what you do with your time tonight, turns you into who you are tomorrow, and the day after that. Look at who you want to be, and start sculpting yourself into that person. You may not get exactly where you thought you'd be, but you will be doing things that suit you in a profession you believe in. Don't let life randomly kick you into the adult you don't want to become."

    – Colonel Chris Hadfield, submitted live
      from space to Reddit, February 17, 2013

If you knew the future, making decisions would be much easier. We have looked at some tools to help you foresee outcomes of decisions. We have looked at ways of getting reliable information to use with those tools. But just having the information about your decision and the tools to make it is not enough. To make good decisions, you need to bring those elements together into an effective process.

For simple decisions with low risk, the process is simple. Just pick a choice. If it doesn't work out, you learn something. It's low risk. But a low degree of confidence in that low risk rating adds complexity. Many people make this mistake. "It's no big deal. I'll just do it. What could happen?" That's a statement declaring low risk. The "what could happen" question is the issue. It implies that they have not performed a thorough likelihood rating. That means there could be great risk that they are ignoring. Acting on their choice without analysing answers to their question would be foolish. You have developed intuition enough to judge that instantly.

Here is the best possible outcome. You respond by giving a high-risk assessment. The person posing the question is trying to entice your engagement. You are now in the role of saving them from risk, thereby exposing your concern for them. They reveal their pleasure at your concern, and their stunt is over. You both laugh.

But what about situations where it is not a stunt and they are serious? Your intuition still feeds you attitudes. You still have a sense of the risk, and of the benefit. You just know without even seeming to think about it. Your explanation is that it is obvious to you. It comes from building up intuition about danger throughout your life. As a toddler, you didn't have that sense. People had to protect you from doing dangerous things. Later, you developed expertise in immediate dangers, like fire and cliffs. As your expertise grew, you built a summary process we sometimes call a learned reaction, good judgment, or even intuition. Now you just "know" a danger when you encounter one. You have combined knowledge and experience to give you reflexive behaviour. Your lifetime of research now pays off in instant judgment. The more you use it, the better it gets. Wouldn't it be nice if you had reflexes like that for decisions that are more complex?

When facing difficult decisions, using a familiar process helps to give you confidence. The more you do it, the more you trust your process. You may have to refine it as you meet new situations, but that makes your process more robust. Over time, you can become both more efficient in going through your process, and more proficient at it. You make the process your own and it becomes part of you. When facing a new decision, you may reach a point where most, or even all, of the choices are part of your awareness instantly. The path to your goal may become quite clear as soon as you grasp the full situation. It can take a long time to develop a sense like that. You can weigh that risk of time investment against the benefit. I would say it is worth working on. Of course, it is your choice.

Building a Path to your Goal

"Every action causes ripples, with consequences both obvious and unforeseen."

– Time traveller "September" in the TV show *Fringe*

Grasping the full situation around a decision is a challenging goal in itself. We tend to race to a conclusion. We jump over facts. Even wanting to move on distracts us in our process. While being able to decide quickly may be a long-term goal, it's more important to make good decisions. You can't make a good decision when you do not have relevant facts. So the key is to accept that it can take time to gather information about your decision, and that's all right. Once you understand the full situation, you may decide quickly or you may agonize over choices. The important thing is to be well informed before deciding. To choose wisely, you should also take a non-emotional, objective look at your goal choices. Choosing what you want right now may not be the best goal for you. Striving to reach a goal can be challenging. This is not a trivial decision.

Goal Decisions

Choosing a long-term goal is often the most complex of decisions. You may face many sacrifices and risks of various types. It could appear as a yes/no decision, or a choice of one out of many. Either way, the decision will commit you to make many other decisions and actions to reach this goal. Let's explore how we might go about it.

What information should we gather first? We need likelihood ratings for consequences and opportunities. We are not simply imagining situations that lead us down a path. If we were just to do that, we could spiral into fantasyland. We could treat as "likely" either all the worst possibilities, or all the best. We need to be realistic in our analysis. We must calmly decide the likelihoods of consequences and opportunities. But on what path should we start looking?

Consider three situations we may encounter. If we already have a goal, we find our path more easily. If we are not sure about what we want, we may need to first visit likely outcomes in our imagination. If our ambition is to explore life, then we can use our values to suggest choices. In all three of these cases, being mindful of a strategy will help guide us. Strategies for these cases could be as follows. To reach our goal, we make choices that enable it. To choose a goal, we imagine ourselves living with each of our choices. To explore life with integrity, we give priority to our values.

Which situation are you in currently? In what new situation might you like to be? Can you state it as a goal? When you describe a goal, it helps make it seem more real. You fill in details, or provide a context. You start imagining what it would be like to experience that goal. Build a description of your goal and discuss it with trusted friends. Let them ask you questions about it. Try writing a description of your goal. Adjust aspects of your description so that it becomes clear and can withstand inspection. Be open to changing your goal's description until you are happy with it. You first thought of your goal as a concept. As you get closer in your mind to that concept, you can describe it better. It's not so much that your goal is changing, but that your ability to describe it is getting more precise. You will feel better about each new level of precision in your description. These steps are bringing you a little closer to your goal.

Secret Tip: **When choosing a goal, write a description of it and then make it even clearer.**

Required Events

Once we have identified our goal, and a strategy to support it, we will work out the path to reach it. Choices make up the path to take us closer to our goal. Often, attaining a goal requires certain events to happen first. These are goal "prerequisites." It is easier to discover these by working backwards from our goal to see what it needs. It's like the old saying, "to put a roof on a house, you first need to put up the walls." Since you will likely have to jump several of these "prerequisite" hurdles before reaching your goal, you might like to make a list of them. Here is one way to diagram them.

We start by looking at any requirements of your goal. Draw a circle representing your goal and label it with the name for your goal. Will you have to have achieved anything before reaching the goal? List all those things outside the circle. Number each item. Check it: "If you complete all those things, then have you achieved your goal?" No? What else does your goal need first? Complete your list. The list is of first-level requirements, or direct prerequisites, for your goal.

Are you ready to achieve all those things on your list right now? If not, you will need a list of other things you must either do or decide, to meet the first-level prerequisites. You may need to make one or more achievements or decisions for each prerequisite. This is the second level out from your goal. Your goal doesn't need you to do these things in particular. You are listing these second level items as ideas or assumptions about how you can meet the direct prerequisites. Create this numbered list further away from your goal than the first list. You may notice several different ways you could meet the prerequisites. You may be ready to start work on some of them right away. For others, you may need to prepare further before you are ready to start. Ask yourself, "How can I get ready to do that?" There may be several ways. That would create a third level of actions or decisions you need, to make progress toward your goal. The further away your goal, the more levels you will have. Stop after you list things you are ready to do now.

You can trace lines between the list levels and through items at each level from your goal. You can follow the lines backward and see what you need to do to meet this prerequisite. You may see a couple of different ways to meet a requirement. If so, you will notice different paths appearing with different approaches or choices. As you show your solutions in more detail, more choices will appear. One path to your goal may be better for you than another is. Don't try to judge it just yet. We are ready to find the best path by first asserting assumptions.

Event Dependencies

These assumptions will be about your path choices and their likelihoods. We are anticipating events, as we discussed above in *Gathering Useful Information*. Let's first take one path to your goal, and start with the item farthest away from the goal. We will start with this item and work through this path toward your goal. We can think of each numbered item on your list as an "event." It could be a decision, an achievement, a payment, or some other kind of action. Like decisions, events can have degrees of risk, consequences, benefits and opportunities. You can list these in a chart like that for decisions. It is similar to the chart in *Figure 4*, but using *Event* instead of *Choice*, and without the Foundation Factors. See *Figure 4a* for an example.

#	Event	Risk	Strength	Likelihood	Consequence	Likelihood	Benefit	Strength	Likelihood	Opportunity	Likelihood

Figure 4a

For each event, ask two questions. First, "How is that going to happen?" Second, "What are the most likely outcomes of that event?" Let's consider the first question first.

We can call the path lines on your list that connect one event to another a "dependency." The second event (moving toward your goal) is dependent on the first one happening. These lines show dependencies. If you miss one event, you cannot move forward on that particular path. If you don't see the answer to the first question about an event, you must create the answer. You will have to create a new event to enable it. Once you have answered the first question above, for all events on your path, you will see all the dependencies linked together.

Likely Outcomes

The second question for each event is, "What are the most likely outcomes of that event?" This is where the chart of *Figure 4a* comes in. The first outcome listed for an event should be the opportunity to move onto the following event.

It is a benefit that we can call the preferred opportunity, or preferred outcome. You can list the follow-on event number as either a Benefit or an Opportunity, depending on the depth of your chart. (Some benefits can yield several opportunities.) If you list it as an Opportunity, you can use "Progress" as the Benefit. Benefit Strength (or Importance) would likely be 10, since this allows you to move on toward your goal. This is your preferred outcome for the event.

Now let's list the most likely outcomes for each event on the path. We listed the preferred outcome because it takes us forward, but we need to see if there are more. What else could happen because of this event happening? How will people respond? What else could it enable? These questions can help us spot "unintended consequences" of this event. We may not want these things to happen. We might be able to keep them from happening, as long as we know they could happen. Now we have our list of possible outcomes for this event. One outcome is the one we want, and others are either nice things that could also happen, or things we want to avoid. The nice things are benefits, or opportunities offered by a benefit. The ones to avoid are the risks, or consequences of a risk.

How likely is each of these possible outcomes? On a scale of

1 to 10, how would you rate the likelihood of the preferred outcome? How would you rate the others? Is there a risk for this event with a high likelihood? What are the most likely benefits and risks? What will you do if they happen? Could one of the risks or consequences block your preferred outcome? If so, this is a critical event, with a critical likelihood. Depending on that likelihood, you may need to consider more options. You may need to find another "Plan B" path to your goal, or start a new sub-project to help ensure your preferred outcome is not blocked.

Repeat this process for each event on the path. Then apply the process to any other paths you have created to reach your goal. Remember that these likelihood ratings are just your initial guesses. We need to improve the accuracy of these initial guesses. We will have to get the facts affecting critical events. We can use the techniques introduced above in *Gathering Useful Information* for support. Highlight the most likely path to your goal. Find the way through that works for you. We may refine it after considering opinions of trusted people. But for now, that is your preferred path.

Weighing Risk and Benefit

You have identified one or more paths with high likelihood.

Look at the preferred outcome likelihoods along your preferred path to the goal. Is it fair to say that the likelihood of reaching the goal is no greater than the lowest likelihood on your path? If you do not get the desired outcome for that event, you cannot continue on that path. You may have to jump to a "Plan B" path. So on this path, reaching your goal is no more likely than succeeding at the lowest likelihood event. Are you interested in increasing its likelihood?

The risks for an event can affect the likelihood of your desired outcome. Some of the risks may not be very important. Strong risks would be disrupting. We need to rate the strength or importance of the risks for events along your preferred path. We can then use that strength with the likelihood of the risk to see if the preferred outcome is affected.

For example, let's say you want to apply for an advertised job that will help you gain skills you need for your path. However, your relative already works there and is against the idea of you having a job, any job. The event is applying for the job. The benefits are several. The preferred outcome is that you can eventually use your new skills to get a better job on your path. Your relative poses at least two risks. First, they could try to block your application by speaking with the interviewers. Then once you are hired, they may try to persuade you to quit. The second risk is not important because you have made up your mind. Even if it is very likely they will do this, it is not important. The first risk is huge. You might never know that they blocked your application for the job. Would they do that? What is the likelihood? If it is very small, the likelihood of your preferred outcome is not affected. If the likelihood is great, with such a huge risk, your preferred outcome is likely doomed. So, great risk with strong likelihood reduces the likelihood of your preferred outcome.

In this example, you devise a plan to control the risk. You will apply for the job without telling your relative, and without listing them on the application. Your plan is to keep them from learning about your application until after you get the job. This will reduce the likelihood of the risk substantially.

This sounds like it could work on paper. In real life, it can get tricky. Perhaps you live with a parent who is in favour of you applying for this job. Their brother is the relative who already works there. Do you ask your parent to keep quiet about your application? You are starting to involve more people in your plan. You are losing influence over its likelihood of success. Perhaps you need another choice. One option might be to have your parent resolve the issue with their brother about you working.

Review the risks along your path with high values for strength and likelihood. Adjust the likelihood of your preferred outcome to be as realistic as possible. Can you devise any plans to reduce the likelihood of these risks? Perhaps you can get some good advice from an expert. If not, this path may not work and you will have to find another one.

Sometimes the benefits justify taking the risks. Recognize that the benefit of your preferred outcome is huge. It enables you to move on to the next step toward your goal. There may be other benefits, as well. Estimate the strength and likelihoods for any other benefits along your preferred path. Review the benefits with high values for strength and likelihood. Compare their likelihoods with the risks for that event. Are any of those risks strong, with high likelihoods? How sure are you of those likelihood numbers? Do the risks outweigh the benefits? Do you think it is worth taking the risk and likely get the benefit? If so, this is still your preferred path. If not, you need to figure out a way to lower the likelihood of the risk. Otherwise, you will have to find an alternate path. Anytime you are facing great risk for an event, it is a good idea to have an alternate path in mind. If you don't get your preferred outcome, you can change paths.

Conflicting Objectives

Choosing a path is not always easy. When one door opens, it seems another one closes. You feel like you are losing an opportunity by making a choice. This is where priorities come in. You have already listed the strength of the benefits along your path. This shows the value to you of these benefits. Review and adjust them again to reflect more accurately their importance to you. Perhaps you feel that even some preferred outcomes are less than a ten. How important to you is each benefit?

Would it be possible to find a path to your goal that went through your most important benefits? If so, the ones you give up would be the less important benefits. That could be wonderful. It is worth a try, but we often face a choice between two desirable events. If they do not have equal benefit strength, the choice is easier. We tend to choose the most beneficial. For a choice between events of equal benefit, it is more difficult. What are their risks? Are we more likely to succeed at one of the events? If so, since they have equal benefit to us, let's choose the one where we are more likely to succeed. We can choose the one with lower risk. We will be happier succeeding at one than perhaps failing at the other.

Secret Tip: **Try to include the most important benefits on the path to your goal.**

Incentives and Threats

Whether you are pursuing a goal or making a decision about something important, you are bound to encounter people trying to persuade you. They will try to get you to do what they want you to do. Let's turn that around for a moment. How do you get someone to do what you want? You could ask them nicely and they might just go along with it. But what if they resist and you still want to sway their decision? That's when incentives and threats come to mind. Some people call it the carrot and stick approach.

When a decision you are making affects others, they may want to influence your choice. They may offer incentives, introduce fear with indirect threats or do both. "We're offering this amazing discount on these last few items, today only. After that, you will have to pay full price, if we have any left." They are combining an incentive to save money with fear that you would lose the opportunity to buy it altogether. We see it all the time: incentive, threat, or both. These tactics try to trigger our emotions into making a quick decision.

Can we use decision-making tools to decide what is best, even under this pressure? We can reduce the situation to terms we already use. Incentives are benefits, or perhaps specific opportunities. If we understand an opportunity, we can describe a benefit for it. We can give the benefit a strength value and a likelihood value. How big a benefit is it? How likely am I to collect the benefit? The threat is a risk, or perhaps a specific consequence. We can describe a risk for a consequence. We can then give the risk a strength value and a likelihood value. How big is the risk? How likely am I to suffer the risk?

Now we have strength and likelihood numbers for both risk and benefit. We can combine these ratings with the Foundation Factors for this choice to get a bigger picture. They are the numbers for Feeling, Values Consistency, and Support for Strategy. Having all these numbers on a scale of 10 will let us think about this decision in a more unemotional way. Let's consider numbers for the last three factors briefly.

Does this decision even relate to your strategy? Here are two strategies we considered earlier. When we have a goal, "To reach our goal, we make choices that enable it." When we are not goal-focused, "To explore life with integrity, we give priority to our values." We may be able to come up with a number for Strategy after a quick reflection. If we consider this decision with our values in mind, we should also be able to choose the Values consistency number. Now let's gauge our Feeling. Remember that, like the other Foundation Factors, we can use minus numbers for negative feelings and zero for no feeling, besides our normal 1 to 10 scale. How do you feel about deciding to do this?

These numbers can crush a choice by themselves, without the risk and benefit numbers. If a choice has no strategy support or consistency with your values, and you feel negative about it, why continue? Is there any benefit that is worth it to you? Considering these three factors first can let us avoid having to judge risk and benefit altogether. Without the foundation, we have no reason to continue.

If a Foundation Factor clearly stops your decision, it may

also give you a small benefit. Sometimes in social situations, we feel we must give a reason for our decisions. It may be appropriate for friends, but you seldom need it for strangers. Still, those pressuring you for a decision have a hard time pandering to your reason when it is a Foundation Factor. Your rejection reasons for each factor would be like this. For Strategy, "I'm not interested. I don't care." For Values, "I don't do that. It doesn't appeal to me." For Feeling, "I don't feel like it. I don't want to." Compare these to reasons about risk or benefit. People often revise their offer when you say the benefit is not big enough, or the risk/cost is too high. They then start to bargain. But they can't bargain around reasons not related to risk and benefit. They can try, but they can only change risk and benefit. They cannot change your strategy, feeling or values.

When decision choices pass the test for Foundation Factors, you must then compare risk and benefit for these choices. Is the benefit large enough? Could it be bigger? We typically want the benefits to outweigh the risks. Think about it and be sure that they do. Is the risk within your "comfort zone?" Sometimes, threats may not even be legal. Talk to an expert if you have any doubts. If the risk is too great, you may want to consider another way to gain this particular benefit. Next, consider the likelihood of receiving the benefit and of suffering the risk. Is there anything you could do to improve the likelihood in your favour? Can you reduce the likelihood of the risk? Can you increase the likelihood of the benefit? Try looking at the situation from another person's point of view. If you can't make a clear decision, get help from those you trust.

Preparing for Consequences

One good way of estimating the strength of a risk is to think about its possible consequences. All risks seem to have consequences. We have already discussed the likelihood of a consequence and even have a way to diagram it. But it is the strength of the consequences, taken together, that contribute to the strength of a risk.

Think of a simple risk, like a payment for a purchase. You know the price, so it is a full likelihood for the risk and the consequence. They are certain. The consequence is that once you pay, you will no longer have the money you paid. Hopefully, the benefit you receive will be worth it. But the consequence of not having that money any more could put you at great risk. A gambler may spend money on a bet, which they were going to use for food and housing. If they lose the bet, that money is gone with no benefit. That consequence makes the risk huge.

Some risks have several consequences. If you see one consequence of a risk, keep looking for any others that might be significant. Unintended and unanticipated consequences have the potential to wipe out all your benefits. Try to see them before you make the decision final. If you find several consequences for a risk, make sure that your risk strength accounts for all the consequences. Take them all together, with their likelihoods, and revise the strength of your risk accordingly.

When you see a list of consequences for a risk, start thinking of ways to avoid or lessen the impact of those consequences. If you were to make that choice and that risk happened, what preparation would help you deal with those consequences?

Sometimes, consequences are time dependent. If you act quickly, you can reduce the damage from the consequence or recover from it. If you know you will likely spill when you water that indoor flower pot, you might think to carry a rag with you to mop it up. If you don't act quickly, the water could ruin all the papers on that desk. Being prepared for quick action saves you from further damage. If you thought about it more, you might come up with a way to avoid the problem in the first place. Is there a way you could prepare better for the consequences of each major risk? What could you do to fix it? Could you have help standing by in case you need it?

If you think about involving other people in helping to avoid or fix damage from a consequence, think of the best people. These would be people well suited to dealing with this kind of harm. They can likely take the least time to treat the issue, and may even have some ideas on how to avoid it. Harm avoided is always much better than injury treated. Include these people in your plan.

Secret Tip: **Prepare for consequences by planning for both avoidance and recovery.**

Dealing with Opportunities

An opportunity opens the way for a future action that you have yet to take. It is not the same as a benefit. Pursuing an opportunity may also deliver a new benefit. A benefit is an improvement in your situation resulting from some action. Knowing the benefit of an opportunity helps you make your choice, since there are large and small benefits. When people talk about opportunities being big or little, they are referring to the benefit. "That's a big opportunity for her." The word "big" doesn't refer to the amount of work she will need to do. It refers to the benefit she will receive when she succeeds. Opportunities are all about promise. They are our link to another event.

You may see several ways to achieve a certain benefit. Each of those ways presents an opportunity with the same benefit. So, several opportunities may share the same benefit. An opportunity might also bring several benefits. If you take advantage of a certain opportunity, like accepting a job offer in a new city, you may enjoy several benefits. Notice that you have to act on the opportunity to receive the benefits.

We see opportunities because we are interested in improving our situation. Wanting benefits drives us to recognize opportunities. We expect the opportunities to make good on their promise and give us access to their benefits. So we are on the lookout for opportunities that might improve our chances. Such opportunities are often time-sensitive and short-lived. We must act on them quickly if we want to pursue them, or else they will be gone. If we could predict their arrival, we could make a decision ahead of time and be ready for them. If we are good at charting a path to a goal, we could imagine which opportunities would be important to us. We could think up ways that different opportunities might arise. We might even be able to see how we could help create just the opportunities we need. We could then enable our own benefits.

Opportunities that Present Themselves

Sometimes we are surprised at new opportunities that seem to arise out of nowhere. They might promise such great benefits that they stun us into disbelief. We cannot act. We cannot consider the proposition or communicate a decision. The concept of "order" seems to leave our mind. We sometimes see this in public marriage proposals. The would-be groom must wait after proposing. He may even repeatedly prompt his soon-to-be fiancé for an answer. Eventually, it comes.

Even when the pressure of time is not an issue, surprising opportunities can still stun us when presented. We tell our friends and family the news about receiving the offer, or discovering the option. We still haven't decided because emotion is keeping us bewildered. We hope that we will be more able to think logically about our decision after talking with them. We could do that and make our decision after getting their initial advice. Another option is to share our emotion with them and say that we will have to think about it calmly when we can take it all in. This will give us time to consider the pros and cons, risks and benefits, along with likelihoods. We can then draw upon each person individually for advice on specific issues we see. We can use their opinions to help refine opinions that we are already forming. We can get their help in doing what is best for us.

Secret Tip: **Form an opinion on opportunities first, and then ask individuals for their advice.**

Revealing Hidden Opportunities

Not everyone recognizes opportunities. People who are not looking for them often pass them by. Opportunities are easier to see if you are expecting them. Sometimes, you have to work at finding them or even enabling them. They can hide behind other opportunities. A low-benefit opportunity can lead you to a new event that links to a big-benefit event. You have to explore the possibilities to see the full picture. Thinking ahead helps you do that.

Just as opportunities often have a time-window that opens and closes, they may also have a quota. They only have room for one person, or some set number. If you see an opportunity first and are ready for it, you can make a claim before someone else does. Those who hesitate may lose out on that opportunity. Those who do not see the opportunity will not compete. Thinking ahead helps you be ready to take the opportunities you hope to find. If you see them, you will already know how to act.

Secret Tip: **When you are hoping for an opportunity, examine possible paths.**

Chapter 6

Acknowledging Feelings

Recognizing Emotion

The rational, thinking part of our brain (the neocortex) does play a role in emotional thought. But a particular type of brain cell (spindle neuron) plays a key role in our high-level emotions and moral judgment. It connects diverse parts of our brain together. These cells communicate emotions and are not involved in rational problem solving. Because of this, we do not have rational control over our emotional response to music or to falling in love. The rest of our brain perceives this as a mystery and tries to make sense out of these high-level emotions. (Kurzweil, 2012, pp. 109-110) This is why filmmakers often feel that almost half of the impact of a movie is the music.

The thinking part of our brain can adjust lower-level emotions though, such as desire and fear. Both desire and fear stimulations can cause us to act without thinking. But we have the brain connections to think about those stimulations before deciding to act. Using thought, we can recognize these emotions, understand and try to control them. Recognition is the key element to this process, providing a gateway to control.

We become excited when we think that we are about to get what we desire. The excitement is part of our thinking process, and can overwhelm us if we let it. We feel anxiety when we think that our fear is about to come true. The anxiety is also part of our thinking process, and can overwhelm us if we let it. So we can think about desires and fears before acting, but they can both overwhelm our thought process if we let them.

To make good decisions when facing desire or fear, we should first recognize and acknowledge them. We could start thinking about them to get a better understanding, and to help us make a decision. If we can expect something to happen, we can better prepare for it. We know that the emotion of excitement or anxiety can take over our thoughtful decision process. Check your Feeling number for each choice and see if it is significant. If it shows high emotion, try to become calmer before you consider this choice. Since that emotion can occur when we think the event is about to happen, we have two choices. We can try to make a good decision before we get too close to the time of the event. That is preferable. We could also try to suppress the excitement or anxiety as it appears, and focus on the decision-making task. That takes mental strength and self-control. Fortunately, we can develop those qualities with practice. Let's look at each of these primal emotions.

Secret Tip: Try to make decisions before you must.

Desire

Desire can become overwhelming, even just by imagining the event. We approach it in our minds and our desire increases. It seems to fill you like a fluid or a gas, and you just want to go with it... Whoa! Shake it off. If you're not careful, you can base all your behaviour on your desire.

Desire is a strong drive, but it does not always help us do what is best for us. If we have time to think before its time to act, we have a chance to consider what is best. We can think about our choices and then decide on our actions. If we can act right away, we get excited. When we are excited, we can easily act without thinking. We go with our desire.

Some people practice making quick decisions. They do this by rehearsing what to do in certain situations. When a similar situation comes up in real life, they go with their training and decide quickly. If they trained well, they do not panic when they see unexpected choices. They quickly analyse and choose. The key to their success is that they stay in their thinking mind. They choose what they *think* is the right choice for the situation. Thinking can be fast.

You do know why you are about to do something. You know that, if you trained to do it that way. Serious sport is like this. You make choices quickly. If you have ever played on a team, you know how fast it can be. You also know when you are about to do something only because you want to. You feel differently about it. Before, just before, you act you know why you are acting. It's true that you can react to a surprise and not know exactly why you did something. But when you choose to act, you know why. You either just wanted to, or you decided carefully. Perhaps you thought about deciding carefully, but then you decided not to be careful. Whoops. You may also have started to decide carefully, and then made your choice without thinking it through. Why? Desire was still attracting your attention towards its choice. When time is short, it is hard to resist excitement.

Thinking can help. Our brains have the connections to recognize desire and think about it before acting. Think of a choice you might face with desire. Go ahead; I'll wait. Maybe the best way to handle desire is to deal with it directly. Who knows, maybe our best choice is to act on our desire. Let's see. What are the numbers? On the plus or minus ten-scale, what would you give this choice for Feeling? That was easy. How consistent is this choice with your values, on that scale? How much does it support a strategy of yours to reach a goal?

Let's talk risk and benefit. What is the biggest risk for this choice? How big on the 1 to 10 scale? What is the likelihood of that risk happening? There must be some benefit to this choice, drawing you to it. Is the benefit big? How big? What is the likelihood of that benefit happening?

Do you have numbers for all that? Even if you didn't write them down, you now have a sense of the numbers. How is this choice looking to you now, by the numbers? Maybe your numbers are wrong. Maybe you should get another opinion. Perhaps you should talk to someone you trust who has experience with this. Let's think about that. To whom would you talk about this?

How is your excitement level now? Sure, the desire may still be there, but you have focused your attention on the numbers of the situation. You have repelled the excitement a little. Is it enough to stay in control? If it is, you get to decide how your life will move forward. Consider the benefit and its opportunity. Will it ever come again? Can you think about it?

When you are feeling desire, think about your choices. Just wanting to move forward towards a goal might shift your desire a bit. The choice that most supports your strategy could inspire some desire too. Think about that one, combined with its score for Values consistency. Thinking more about a choice with good scores for Values and Strategy factors might help. You might decide to improve your Feeling score for that choice. Of course, the Feeling score for your desired choice is still looming. But all things considered, thinking can help you make a better choice.

Fear

"To conquer fear is the beginning of wisdom."

– Bertrand Russell

A strong person can admit their fear, and face it. You can do that too. Your brain connections let you think about fear that you recognize. Fear comes from the outside, and anxiety comes from within. So, the key to facing fear is to think about the source of your fear, and yet not become nervous about it. What is the risk this fear brings with it? Is there more than one risk? List them. Pick the first one. We can already assign a strength value to the risk. With more thought, we can assign a value for likelihood, too. Since the fear we are talking about is coming from a choice we are to make, we could describe consequences. Are there consequences connected with a risk of this choice? What is the likelihood of each consequence? Is there any way to reduce the likelihood of likely consequences?

Let's consider the likelihood of the strongest risk. How likely is it? How sure are you that it's that likely? Can you get another opinion on its likelihood? Do you both agree? Can either of you see a way to lessen the likelihood of this risk? Are other choices available to avoid taking this risk?

Have you explored those choices? Have you discussed them with experienced people you trust?

Thinking about this situation has now become a small project. You are thinking about it in several different ways. You have examined options and alternatives. You have discussed it with one or more people you trust. You may even have assembled a small team to help you. The fear is still there, but it is not as awful as it first was. You now see it as part of a situation that you are trying to deal with in a careful way. You have support from others who want to help you with their experience and guidance. The fear is not so scary when you start to accept possible choices for your decision.

External Pressures

Feeling pressured to make a choice is an uncomfortable situation. One type of pressure is to hurry up and make your choice. Choosing quickly is easier in a familiar situation. Even then, the pressure is unwelcome, and distracting. If the risks and benefits are high, demanding more quiet time is essential. If you are not familiar with the choices, choosing quickly could be just a guess. Good decisions are not based on guesses. So, find an ally who can keep the pressure away from you, and go through a more comfortable decision-making process.

Another type of pressure is to make a certain choice. We're not talking about threats, or incentives, since we dealt with them earlier. This pressure is more socially acceptable. It is open and can even appear to be caring. It can come from friends, family, school staff or prospective employers. It can be to accept the opportunity of a certain offer. It can come from friends who want you to do something dubious with them. It can be to join a group or team. They apply the pressure in a way to make you feel sought-after. This is social pressure to accept an offer.

Our normal analysis using risk, benefit, values and feeling still applies to these decisions. But the risk and its consequences seem intense due to the social pressure. It can cloud your judgment. Someone who has been through this before and is not feeling this emotional pressure may be able to give good advice. After you set numbers for the strength of risk and benefit, and for their likelihoods, find some help. Ask them to tell you what they think the numbers would be. Also, consider consequences and ask about numbers for likelihoods. Outcomes you imagine under social pressure can balloon up. They are often not as bad as you think, and less likely to happen. It is not always that way, but the risk may be lower and less likely. Remember to set numbers for this choice's consistency with your values, and for your feeling about it. Think about this decision's effect further out into the future. Having perspective from a future view can often help make your priorities clear.

Courage

"Feel the fear and do it anyway." ®

      – Susan Jeffers

Doing what you think is right in the face of risks, such as social ridicule, threats and personal sacrifice, takes courage. Even if you have made a good decision, it can still be hard to act on it. Yet, you can develop skills that strengthen your resolve to "do it anyway" (Jeffers, 2006). These include:

- confidence,

- organizational skills, and the

- ability to influence others.

Imagine having loads of those skills. All these take time to develop, but just identifying them as being desirable can help you. When you see opportunities to build these skills, you can make a choice to take action and strengthen your abilities. These are strategic skills, and they can help you reach your goals. Imagine combining the ability to make good decisions with these skills. Take a moment. Do you feel the courage? It gives you strength.

How would you feel about creating a "standing strategy" to improve these skills whenever you can? You would always have this strategy going on, and you would apply it when it fits. The strategy could be like this. "If I take opportunities to improve skills in confidence, organizing, and influencing others, I will become more courageous." It is the courage-building strategy. When you consider a choice for a new opportunity, you can set a number for its support of your "courage-building" strategy. If that number is high, think about increasing your number for Benefit strength. That kind of opportunity could help you a lot. Let's look at ways you might build these three skills.

Confidence

Planning can go a long way to bolster confidence. Preexperiencing the steps you will take because of a decision allows you to fine-tune the details of what to do and what to expect. Mind experiments can help you become confident, playing out options and considering the outcome. When you do act, you are more confident because you are in somewhat familiar territory.

If your mental projection shows you need an ability you are normally weak in, that is a useful thing. It means you have identified a specific area to focus on and improve. Now you have a sub-project with a clear-cut goal: improve that area of performance. Play it out both ways. You could keep the area of weakness and avoid the choice that requires it. You could overcome the weakness and follow the choice that uses the newly bolstered ability. Which outcome is better? What is the cost? Is it worth it?

There is a hidden benefit when choosing to improve in an area of perceived weakness. Your improvement builds confidence. Be sure to acknowledge it step by step. Celebrate your small successes. Commit yourself to your goal. Take the next step. Confidence is becoming your shadow. The stronger it becomes though, the more you should leave it in the shadows. Others value humility in you, not confidence. The confidence is just for you. (Chamorro-Premuzic, 2013, p. 70)

Organizational skills

Being well organized is a gift to you yourself. You don't do it so you can impress others. You stay organized to avoid frustration and feel effective when you want to do anything. You know where your things are and you know their condition. You use your memory to find things, and you feel in control.

It's easy to get organized and it is easier to stay that way. Be mindful. Decide what the best place for a thing is. Keep it there. Use it. Remember where it "lives." Return it there. It is your thing and you are responsible for being able to find it when you want it. Use your memory. Think when you put something down. Take a mental snapshot. Remember to put it away properly. Be happy about it.

Another advantage of being organized is that you tend to prepare for events. You assemble what you will need to do tasks you take on. It doesn't matter if you are just following a recipe to prepare a dish, or building a structure. Assembling your supplies and tools ahead of time, means they will be ready right when you need them. You don't have to go off to look for things, and maybe not find them. You feel more empowered and ready to go.

Making a plan helps to prepare you for the event. The process organizes you. When you have a plan, you feel ready to complete it. So what's the best way to plan? You can plan to explore, or you can plan to reach a goal.

If you are planning an exploration, start with what you already know and plan to move towards what you don't know. Prepare by listing things you might expect to encounter and make sure you can deal with those. Ensure that you will have access to tools, supplies and information you might need. Choose someone to keep in touch with, who is not exploring with you. List the milestones that would mark an achievement for you. Decide your limits ahead of time. Will you go beyond each milestone with a separate exploration at another time, or just continue on from there? List the conditions under which you would or would not continue. Set a time limit for your exploration in case you do not reach a milestone. You can always plan to do it again. Review your progress on a regular basis. Document what you learn.

Planning to reach a goal starts by clearly defining the goal and what reaching it looks like. Working backwards, you can list milestones that will mark your progress when you move forward. For each milestone, list the resources and the skills you will need to get there from the previous one. Make a time estimate on how long that will take. The work toward some milestones could happen at the same time. That would save time overall, and you would reach your goal sooner. Decide which milestones those are, and see how many people that would take. List the skills and resources for those milestones and find suitable people to do those things. These people could be service providers, such as consultants or businesses. If many of the needed skills are the same, you could add team members. They could take on several of these milestones as smaller projects.

Add up the cost for all the resources you have identified to reach your goal. Add the cost of external service providers. Add up the time for projects of team members. If you are paying your team, compute a cost based on time. Consider other ways of rewarding them, too. This is your initial plan. If you had the needed resources, access to the right people, and the time to do it, would you do this project? You know the benefit, and now you have estimated the risk. You are in a better position to declare likelihoods for each. If you lead this project, you will have to make sure that the team makes progress towards each milestone. They must be on time and within the budgeted resources. If they stray from the plan, will you be able to spot the slippage before it gets too big? Will you help people achieve their targets? Will you pester and annoy them into leaving? How will you make progress after that? These are all extra risks.

One great way to answer all these questions is to practice over a longer period. Create a new small project with a goal to do it all yourself. Identify the milestones and plan it out. Do the project and keep notes on your milestone achievements. How was your time estimate? Did you spend money? How close was your budget estimate? Learn from those decisions and experiences. Plan a bigger project that would use a very small team. The risks and benefits should be enough to motivate the team members, but not enough to cause a lot of grief if things go wrong. Keep notes again. How did you do? What more did you learn? Are your estimates getting more realistic? Do another one.

Even without projects, we have opportunities every day to test ourselves and get better. Ask yourself some questions. How long will that take? How much will that cost? It is much easier for us to prepare for situations when we have a good idea of what will happen and what it takes to do it. Organizational skills come from preparing for the expected. Do it often and your skills will get better.

Influencing others

Do you trust your friends? Do they trust you? Why should they? Why should they not? It's all about your track record. Did you let them down in the past? Do they just put up with you? Were you there for them when they needed you? Do they value your friendship? Do you value theirs? These things count when other information is missing. This is how most people make decisions when not enough information is available. They trust their friends. Of course, they trust some more than others.

You can have two major things to sway people's opinion. First is the skill of communicating facts clearly. Second is, a lot of friends who trust you. When you put facts together in a way that makes sense to people, you can then express your opinion and they will listen. Not all will agree with you perhaps, but they will hear your advice. Those who know you will likely agree, or at least admit you have a valid point. Those who do not know you will consider the facts you presented, along with other information they already had. If your opinion makes sense, like the way your presented facts did, they will consider it too.

Not everyone who hears your facts will already know them. Some will want to verify your facts with their sources, often with their trusted friends. Missing information makes a decision more difficult for people. It can take a lot of work to go and find that missing information. Instead, they may talk to your friends, "How well do you know this person, and do you think they're right? What do you think about this?" You want friends who trust you.

You build trust over time. You do for your friends what you have promised to do. You don't promise if you can't follow through. Instead, you explain why you can't promise and how you feel about it. You make sure you are there for them when they are in emotional need. You also celebrate with them. You share your view of things with them, and they know they can count on you. They trust you.

Your friends all have their own lives, but they listen to you. If you want to, you can influence them. If you are a good friend, you will influence them in a way that is good for them. They will recognize it, even if they are not ready to act. They appreciate you wanting the best for them. They trust you more because of it. You have more courage because of them. It's the best kind of courage because it comes from trust in your personal relationships.

Exposure

You feel exposed when there is no trust. Anything you do or say could be used in any way, even against you. This is not a friendly situation. It may be cordial and seem friendly, but you feel exposed to danger. You need to weigh risk and benefit carefully, and pay attention to your values while you track your feeling. Try to avoid immediate decisions if you can, and get more time to think clearly. It is not quite fear that you feel, and there are no threats, yet. This could even be a situation of your own making. A mistake you made may have exposed you to unnecessary risk. Try not to panic.

Think about the numbers. How big is the risk? What is its likelihood? Who is an expert with experience in situations like this? Can you get their help? What is your time frame?

How did you get into this situation? Did you see it coming? Was there once trust that is now lost? Can you rebuild the trust? Did you enter this situation carrying secrets that form your risk? What can you do to lessen the risk? Would it be worth it? What do the numbers say?

The loss of trust is one of the worst feelings. It hits you in the gut. Try very hard not to do that to someone. When you feel it, you must make a decision. Either you misread it, or someone else made a decision that destroyed it. Your choices are to rebuild the trust or back away and withdraw from the relationship.

Other people do make bad decisions. Sometimes they are purposeful, and sometimes they realize their mistake. If the other person feels no remorse, and that it was not a mistake, back away. If you do not do that, more pain awaits you. If they regret their mistake, they will want to rebuild the trust they just lost. They will use the word "please" many times. You, however, are still exposed. So, you need to avoid immediate decisions if you can, and get more time to think clearly. If you eventually decide to rebuild the relationship's trust, it is more difficult than with a stranger. You are starting from betrayal, which is negative trust. Just getting back to neutral trust will be hard. This will likely take much longer than it did the first time. Consider the benefits carefully, because you would be making a long-term investment.

Did you walk into a situation of exposure? Did you make a mistake and reveal or do something that could be used against you? It is not that trust was lost. You knew it would not be there in the first place. When exposure is your own doing, you can only try to fix the issue and learn from the experience. You may not be able to recover by yourself. You may need the help of an expert. The risk may be high and the cost higher. Education is sometimes expensive. Make sure you learn from it.

Recognizing Intuition

Intuition can give you great freedom, if you use it properly. Not only does it save you a lot of time, but it can also encourage you to take certain new opportunities. Choices might appeal to you through properly sensed intuition, but may not have high benefit numbers. With extra analysis, you might find that these choices lead to others with greater benefits. You might not normally see this benefit hidden behind the lack-luster choice. Intuition can lead you to look there.

To use it properly, you need to know a little bit about how intuition works and how to detect it. It votes on choices you are considering, but you have to know how to "hear" it. It can sometimes present its vote as a "gut feeling," but not always. You have to be able to tell it apart from other feelings. It comes as a feeling that is not emotional. Since this might sound strange, let's look into it further.

When someone comes to your door and you open it, how long does it take you to recognize your friend? Do you ponder the issue and go through a rational decision-making process? When you hear the beginning of a familiar song, how long does it take you to come up with the next note? Do you think through several choices for the note and choose the best fit? In both these cases, your brain delivers an answer without involving the thinking part of your mind. It does this through its special pattern-matching power. Give it part of a pattern and it will come up with the whole thing, as long as it is familiar with it. It can do this with situations too. "I know how this is going to end," your friend says. How do they know? They patterned-matched the situation and predicted the outcome. They could have also figured it out by using a reasoning process. But if they were familiar with that situation, their brain likely just came up with the answer right away.

So your brain has the answer to a pattern you are considering. Now it has to tell you about it. How does it communicate to your thinking mind? Also, can your thinking mind communicate to it and tell it to do this pattern-matching trick? You can ask it to do this. The problem comes when you keep shouting at it to come up with an answer and you give all your focus to that. Your attention stays on the asking. You have no attention left to put on perceiving the answer. This causes a delay in your conversation, or thought process. To cover that delay you say, "Oh, it was right on the tip of my tongue." You glimpsed that the answer was ready and you almost knew what it was. Then your attention went back to asking for it again, and away from perceiving it. You have to stop asking for it. You are jamming the system with your noise. "Oh well," you say, "it will come to me later."

How do you feel when you later realize the answer to the pattern recall you assigned to your brain? Do you feel good? Do you feel satisfied? Do you feel happy? Do you feel encouraged? Looking back on it, how did you know that the answer had shown up? How did you know that this thought, that just occurred, was connected to the quest on which you had sent your brain? Did you pattern-match, once again? Did you recognize the missing puzzle piece that you were looking for earlier?

This is how your brain tells you. It has found the answer in what seems like no time. The hard part is trying to get you to "listen" to the answer. That feeling that you get when an answer "comes to you," is special. If you were trying hard to remember, the feeling is loaded with other feelings too, like relief. If you were hardly trying at all, you might just ignore the feeling, since it is so subtle. There is no emotion with it, yet it is still a feeling. That's the feeling of pattern-matching telling you the answer to what you seek. That is intuition knocking on your door. Remember it. Recognize it. Become aware of how it is different from other feelings. It is not desire, and it is not fear. It is its own feeling. It is the feeling of "knowing."

Secret Tip: Learn to "listen" to your intuition.

Intuition and Trust

Once you start to recognize votes that your intuition is placing, you can start to track its recommendations. How do things turn out when you follow them? Are they worthy of your trust? You will become better at recognizing the votes themselves the more you track them. Practice improves your performance. When you consider setting a number for your Feeling factor on a new choice, think about your intuition's vote. It can be positive or negative. How strongly do you feel, intuitively, about this choice? You could easily have no intuitive vote on a choice, for which you should set a zero Feeling. Once you start using intuition for your Feeling factor, you can track your intuition more objectively. This will help you to trust it more appropriately. Taking emotion out of the Feeling factor doesn't remove fear and desire from your analysis. Benefit and Opportunity reflect Desire. Risk and Consequences reflect Fear. Having intuition as the Feeling factor will help you build confidence in your intuitive judgment.

Keep in mind that your intuition needs patterns of experience to be the best at its job. When you were a child with no experience, you had no patterns to guide you. As you live your life, you will get more experience that feeds your intuition. This is normally a great thing. But in some situations, it can cause a problem with your intuition. For example, consider a person who was in a bad environment. They might learn from experience that any seeming act of kindness toward them carried a terrible price. Once they left that environment for a healthy one, they would carry their experiences with them. Their intuition would vote against accepting any show of kindness. Their pattern matching would predict a bad outcome. Experience would direct their natural tendency. With a lot of work, they could figure out their new environment by using a reasoning process. But their intuition would not free itself of the cautious votes, since the memories would linger. In this new safe environment, they could not trust their intuition for a while.

We know that various factors can bias your intuition (Kahneman, 2011).We can try to watch out for this and not act impulsively. Once again, thinking will help us to make a good decision.

When applying intuition, remember that it is giving you a vote in our framework. It is an important vote, but so are the Foundation Factors of consistency with your Values, and support of your Strategy goals. You don't have to do only what your intuitions votes for. Intuition works best when the environment for your choice is compatible with that of your past. If you change to an environment not consistent with your past, you may need to change your treatment of intuition. If you have never been deceived, you may not intuitively spot deceit in someone trying to persuade you. If you are used to deceit and then move into a better environment, it is okay to apply caution at first when your intuition is wary. Let yourself learn from positive experiences, as you build new trust in your intuition. Taking more small risks in an improved environment could provide some wonderful surprises.

Secret Tip: **Intuition works best in a familiar environment.**

If your mind could tap into many more experiences, wouldn't it be better at finding matching patterns? Psychiatrist and psychotherapist Carl Jung researched a concept he called the "collective unconscious." He found that in certain situations we might have unconscious access to the sum of humanity's experience. (Paul O'Brien, 2015) Accessing that resource involves identifying a goal and noticing synchronistic events. You need practice and trust in the process to see results. Those who do claim that their connection to this "Infinite Intelligence" gives them what they need to be creative, productive, successful and happy.

Chapter 7

Sequences and Time Factors

One thing leads to another. Even if we are not seeking a goal on some path, things happen when we make decisions. Other things happen whether we make a decision or not. The world keeps moving. If we ponder a decision too long, our decision may not apply any more. Our window of opportunity has closed, and the train has left the station. Time is usually an important factor in decision-making.

Even when we have lots of time to decide, we often must decide which thing is better to do first. Sometimes it is obvious that you can't do one thing without first doing another. Other times, you could do things in either order, but the results would be different. Good decisions consider sequence and time.

Recognizing Cause and Effect

It is not likely that you will know all the ways your action will affect others. You make a decision hoping that your action will produce a certain outcome. Often that outcome is to benefit you. Sometimes you hope to bring benefit to someone else. In all cases, there are likely other effects of your action. Those effects will cause other actions, and so on. You can't possibly know all those, and certainly not in advance of taking your action. Some call these "unintended consequences," but they could also include "unintended benefits." You might imagine some, but not all.

The motivation for your decision is your desired outcome. This is your intention. You should consider a few other effects that your decision might have, but you will have to act to be sure of them. Since actions are final and we can't step back in time, we check the likelihood of high risks and consequences first. If we do this in a responsible way, we include effects of our risks and consequences on others. You can think of it as a "safety protocol." We want to avoid harmful surprises.

Secret Tip: **Consider effects of your risks and consequences on others when likelihoods are high.**

Surprising benefits though, we want to embrace. If we discover a new benefit after we take action, we are usually quite happy about it. "Wow, I didn't I see that coming." "Why," would be a good question. It might be time to review your decision-making process and see why you missed that benefit. Still, it is a good thing, so don't take it so hard. Remember, you can't foresee all outcomes. Just be ready to grasp them when they happen. Don't stay in shock so long that you can't act on the new beneficial opportunity. That would be a waste. Stay agile. The world keeps moving.

Setting Sequence and Priorities

Do you do the most important things first? Maybe you first deal with all the less important things to allow full focus on the important ones. How do you assign priorities to decisions about related things? Do you make your decisions in a certain sequence or in order of highest priority first? Let's consider two cases.

Setting priorities means first deciding how important each decision is. A decision can be important for a couple of different reasons. The first case could be a decision that other actions are depending upon, regardless of its outcome. It blocks progress until it's decided. That could make it a very important decision. Other people seem to care more about having the decision made than they do about the decision itself. It becomes a high-priority decision, which you should make soon.

Another reason for a decision to be important is that its choices have strong benefits or risks. There are major opportunities or possible consequences depending on this decision. In this case, people may express great concern about the consequences and question the benefits. Others want to move ahead with the benefits and downplay the possible consequences. This is an important decision, yet one that seems worth the wait to get right. It seems to be more important to have it be a good decision than to have it made right away. The priority here is to have a good decision.

In the first case, the priority is to have a decision made. In the second case, the priority is to have a good decision. It is easy to confuse the two, and many people do. Some decisions have elements of both. A decision can have strong benefits and risks attached, and it is blocking other actions. Don't let this condition fool you. This is the second case. You can easily show this with a couple of questions. Would you prefer to make a bad decision right now? Are you willing to wait for an excellent decision? Answering "no" and "yes" respectively means that it is the second case. Any other set of answers means you have an agenda that you are promoting.

Once your priorities are clear it is easier to see the best order for your decision-making.

Secret Tip: **A decision with high risk and big benefit justifies the time to get it right.**

Making Timely Decisions

What do you want to do today? That question has some complex parts. One of them is the urgency of accomplishing something before the end of today. Coming up with a list of things you would like to do sometime, could be a fun exercise. Requiring that the list be only of things for doing today adds complexity. What is your current situation? How much of the day is left? Who might be available to take part? There could be many more questions.

Most choices you make relate to time in some way. It is up

to you to consider that relationship when making a good decision. Often there comes a time when your decision is required. After that time, your decision doesn't much matter. Time constraints on a decision should affect its priority for you. If you can see that you will have to make a decision in the future, you may have an advantage. You might be able to start your decision process before the decision is upon you. This would give you extra time to decide.

If the need for a decision surprises you, then you are likely going to rely on intuition for your choice. If you have lots of experience with the subject, then you have a good basis for a quick choice by pattern-matching the past. If you are in unfamiliar territory with this subject, your challenge is to find enough time to think through your decision. If it is not available, your choice will likely be that of chance. In that case, your chance of a good decision will be about 50%. The lesson here is to get ready before putting yourself in a position where you must make a quick decision. Become familiar with the new environment and situations. Learn with small risks and gain experience. Try to move from quick decisions of 50% good, to always-good decisions.

Quick decisions often increase their own risk. Since you

don't have time to consider all the possible outcomes, you base your choice on experience. If this situation happens to be unique, it may not fit your experience profile. Then the risk of you making the wrong decision increases. If you have time to spend on a decision, use the vote of your intuition along with other factors. Instead of basing your decision on only intuition, also consider how each choice fits in with your values and your goal. With even more time, analyse the risk and benefit numbers too. What are the strengths and the likelihoods? With practice, you can do this whole analysis quite quickly. It is slow to begin with, but you can improve your time and keep your decision quality high.

When to Act

If you do not carry out your decision, it is like you never made it in the first place. It is the same as making the non-decision. But there may be a better time than another to act on your decision. You have made the decision, now think how it would be if you applied it at different times. You must act before any deadlines, but is it best to move on it right away? When would be the best time to act? Choosing just the right time is an intuitive process. (Paul

O'Brien, 2015) Make sure that it feels right to you.

Effective timing can be quite beneficial to your actions. See if timing would help each of your significant decisions, and try to arrange your schedule to take advantage of a time benefit. Try to position yourself in the right situation at the right time.

Once you act on your decision, you will move forward on that path. So try to be sure about your choice before you announce it to others and take action. If you were successful, you created a safe place to try out options with people you trust. Once you leave this Decision Island, it is very difficult to change your mind and go back. Other people may make their own decisions to accommodate the one you announce. Changing your mind after you make your decision brings frustration. If you think you must reconsider, first analyse the risks and benefits of changing your decision. Once people have heard your decision, changing your mind may include costs to relationships that are hard for you to see. Put your energy into making your decision a good one that you don't need to change.

Chapter 8

Learning from Past Decisions

There are two traps we might fall into when looking at past decisions. One is that we are too hard on ourselves, and the other is that we fail to accept what we did. In the first case, we are likely to limit our growth by setting unnecessary restrictions on our future behaviour. In the second case, we fail to grow because we deny that we set out to do something and then did it.

The whole point of learning from your past is to grow in a direction that you choose. So you need to be realistic when you think about what you did, why you did it, and effects of the outcome. If you regret a past decision, resolve to think clearly about how to improve decisions in the future. Don't just react with a vow to "never do that again." Think about what you could do differently to produce a new outcome. Don't just try to avoid an outcome.

If the outcome was not the best, try to stand back and look at how it happened from the point-of-view of an uninterested party. Try to be objective. Identify the actors, but keep from identifying with them. See who did what, and when. If the actor who looks like you did something, let them do it in your mind. Wonder why they did it and wonder if they expected the outcome they got. If you think the outcome surprised them, look for their failures to think ahead or learn more about the situation. Look at any motivations for their decision that they might be hiding, even from their self. See if their surprise at the outcome is genuine, or if there may be a hint of expectation and satisfaction. No one will know that you see these things. It is all in your mind. Can you learn from what this person did? If a situation like this comes up for you in the future, what steps do you think you could take to get the best outcome? Now accept that you could have done better this time, and resolve to do better next time. Grow in a better direction. Think of it as a goal.

Secret Tip: **Make your actions produce an intentional outcome.**

Harvesting Hindsight

Learning about ourselves can be difficult. It is easier sometimes to observe the behaviour of our friends. We seem too close to ourselves to see our own behaviour. We do see the reaction of others to our behaviour, though. We can remember that, even if we would sometimes rather forget. Thinking about reactions people have had to us can help remind us of events. Our actions triggered those reactions in other people. If we think through those events, we realize that we preceded our actions with thoughts and decisions. Even though we might call some of them thoughtless decisions, it's not exactly true. If we are honest with ourselves, we knew what we were doing. In low-risk situations, we can call it just being silly. In high-risk situations, it's called being stupid.

Being silly in a safe environment is fun. We can try out odd ideas and behaviours to see how it feels and how certain other people relate to it. We are learning in a safe environment through play. As long as the other people are okay with you playing, it is a great process. If you keep the ability to be playful when appropriate, you will have a great asset throughout life. Play allows you to set up situations and explore possible outcomes of your decisions. You get immediate feedback. It works well for interesting situations.

Unfortunately, it is rare to find a safe environment for serious play. To learn about serious decisions, we use thoughtful reflection. We examine the experiences of others and ourselves, and use our imagination. We can play it over in our minds to see how we might have made a different decision. We can become certain that our actions were consistent with our decision. We can examine the effects of our actions and compare those to what we expected. We can discuss our analysis with trusted friends to get a different perspective. Through all this, we are learning.

Reflecting on good decisions is as important as examining bad ones. Knowing what went right is important for reinforcing that thought process. It also has an emotional benefit. It helps to increase your confidence when facing new decisions. Often when you look back at a decision, you will see things that you did well, as well as things that you should have done better. Try to learn from both. If you do that, you will improve your ability to make good decisions.

Learning to Recognize a Pattern

Sometimes we do things without making a conscious decision. Habits are like that, whether good or bad. Other times we consider our choices briefly, then decide and act right away. We like the familiar. If a choice takes us into familiar territory, it attracts us. We tend to go with that. It may not have been the best decision for us, but we knew what to expect so we chose it anyway. The next time we face that decision, we will likely decide the same way. The decision has become "comfortable."

Coming to the same decision point and deciding the same way every time, describes a pattern of behaviour. These are not quite habits, but are things we always do the same way. This is great for carefully thought out procedures, as we explore below. But for decisions that we have not carefully thought out, we could be acting against our own best interests. Do you want to weaken and depress yourself every day, just because the choices are familiar to you? Over time, you will feel stronger and happier if you know your patterns of behaviour are good for you. If we identify these patterns and review them, we have a chance to keep the good ones and fix the flawed ones.

First, we have to learn how to spot our patterns. The ones that are not very good for us are sometimes the easiest to see. The next time you find yourself mentally cringing at your situation, ask yourself if you have done this before. Maybe you are crossing the street in the middle of the block, dodging cars, when one of them honks because it almost hit you. Whoops. Do you usually do this? Maybe you have just said, "Yes" when someone offers you something that is not very good for you. Do you always say "Yes?" These are the almost automatic choices we make that form our pattern of behaviour. It is at these points we need to make a mental note to review these patterns.

We also do some things on a regular basis that we have decided are good for us. When the opportunity arises, we choose without question because we already decided it was good. The opportunities will depend on your lifestyle. They could be about exercise, eating choices, staying hydrated, or getting enough sleep. We need to celebrate ourselves when we realize we are choosing to be better.

Whenever you realize you are repeating behaviour, pause for a moment. Recall whether you have reviewed and approved this pattern. If so, celebrate with a smile. If not, make a note to have a talk with yourself soon. You are going to find a way to make yourself better.

Applying What We Learn

As hard as it is to admit to ourselves that we could do things better, it sometimes seems harder to change. If it were a minor change, you would think it should be easier. You have taken a hard look at decisions of the past and figured out what you could do to improve your future. But let's face it. You don't really know for sure. The only way to find out for sure whether your change in choice is going to be better is to do it. Maybe it won't be better. Maybe some unforeseen factor will show itself and complicate things for you. You had better try this option out and see if it is actually better. Try it once, anyway, at least to find out if it is better. If it turns out to be better, you can decide then whether to continue doing things the new way or not. At this point, you only have to commit to doing it the new way once. So, the next time this choice arises, can you do it the new way? Please?

Chapter 9

Decisions for You and Us

Who should benefit from your decisions? It is important to know what benefits will come to you from your decision. That helps you make it. But when the benefits will affect a whole group of people, do you decide in the same way? If it is a significant decision you may still consult with experts, and talk to people you trust about the options. But do you talk to the group who will benefit, before you make the decision? Should they be involved in the decision, or is it only yours to make? Should you surprise them? Are you sure that they all would like this benefit? Could it create a problem for them?

If you did talk to them, would you tell them that you were about to decide, or would you just offer them the benefit? If they were to accept your offer, you would act. If they decline the offer, you would not act. Your decision then becomes about whether to make an offer that you would stick to.

Let's consider decisions that will likely have hefty risks. If those risks are to a group, should you involve them before deciding? Would you put that group of people at risk by making a decision in private? How would you feel about someone putting a group you belonged to at such risk? So are you saying that if a large risk to a group were likely, for a decision you were making, you would first talk to them? I'm sure they would appreciate that. If the risk to the group were a little smaller, would you still talk to them before deciding? So when is it okay to make a decision privately that puts a group of people at some risk?

If we consider a group that you might belong to, our position may change a bit. Let's give the group some structure and call it an organization. Inside, it has people in certain positions. Everyone knows ahead of joining this organization that each position plays an important role. They expect people in those roles to make decisions that will affect the whole organization. People all agree to have these decision-makers deal with important issues. It frees them up to focus on doing other things. If you are in a decision-making role, you may have to make decisions that affect many other people. They trust you to make good decisions, and not to come to them as a group before making them all. Being part of the group changes the way you look at these decisions. They are decisions that affect you and others too.

Doing it Your Way

When you make decisions on behalf of other people, your process can be the same as usual. You can still use the approach discussed in the previous chapters. It is just that the risks and benefits are not all on you. If the other people have a goal, you can judge how well each choice supports their strategy. You may feel that the other two Foundation Factors present issues: Feeling and Values. If you know the other people well, or if they have stated values, you can more easily rate choices for consistency with their values. Organizations often state their values, so that should help you. That leaves Feeling.

Feeling is still a valid factor for you to rate. How do you feel about this choice? Even using intuition will work when judging on behalf of others. When we decide for ourselves, we often entangle Feeling with our emotion about the choice. Even though we are deciding for others, our feeling about a choice is still valid. The Feeling we need to rate is how well this choice will work out. If we are experts in the subject, we have valid intuition about it. If not, we still have some experience to draw upon. The feeling about the choice comes from the decision-maker. It is not the feeling of those who might benefit or be at risk. A group leader makes decisions based on their own experience.

For group decisions, the group members are the decision-makers. Each of them can rate the benefits, risks, values alignment and strategy support. They can also rate their Feeling about the choices. Usually, a simple vote from each member then settles the decision. If you like numbers, the group might like you to show them the average, and perhaps mean, of their ratings. If they split the simple vote, a more detailed look at the position of group members could help their thought process.

Using Procedures

Figuring out the best way to do things all the time can be difficult. It requires constant decision-making. Finding the best way by making the best decisions can involve a lot of trial-and-error. Once you have figured it out, however, you don't ever have to decide again. You can just do it the same way. You have invented a time-tested procedure that works. Just follow that procedure and everything will work out fine, as long as there are no surprises. Usually, there are no surprises because you already encountered them and made them part of the procedure.

One of the great things about procedures is that you can describe them as a series of steps. It is like following a recipe. If you write down the steps, you can forget about the procedure and it will still work. You just need to follow the written steps the next time you want to do that thing. You can also have others follow the procedure, and they will likely get the same job done in the same way. They just have to be good at following procedures. Someone who is good at following procedures may think they have found a better way to do it. What makes them good is that they still follow your procedure, and wait until later to suggest their idea to you. You may decide to revise and re-test your procedure, or not. It is your procedure and it does work.

Secret Tip: **When you have decided the best way to do something, formalize it as a procedure.**

Decisions in Management

Your first exposure to management will likely be by observing it. You may see how someone manages others, or have them as your manager. You may wonder why they do not do the same work as the people they manage. It is because they devote their time to ensuring that their team achieves its goals on time. Drivers, pilots and ship captains have a somewhat similar role. Their job is to ensure their group gets safely to its destination on time. Like them, managers make a plan and then guide the work of their group to meet their goals. Along the way, they must make more decisions when they encounter surprises. They try to avoid delays, and make up for them if they occur. They try to do all this by using only the resources they thought they would need at the beginning.

Managers usually report to other people who judge their achievements. These people feel that managers who meet their targets on time and within given resources are good at their job. If you have a manager, you may base your feeling about them on different factors. Generally, good managers are those who make good decisions. If you consistently make good decisions, you will likely make a good manager.

But great managers go beyond making good decisions. When it comes time to act on those decisions, they have already prepared their team for what is coming. They have done this in a way that lets every team member feel valued, and ready to contribute. Team members enjoy working within the team because of its management. They feel their needs are met, and welcome new challenges with trust in their manager. The great manager builds on this trust, and uses it to help them make good decisions.

Leadership Opportunities

While managers strive to ensure the job gets done right, leaders must ensure that it is the right job. (Alex Lowey, 2004, p. 279) The manager watches quality, and the leader gauges validity. Leaders decide direction of the organization, and provide the passion that drives it. Leaders are concerned with vision, direction and opportunity. They rely on managers to determine the "how" and "when" of meeting that opportunity. Time limits sometimes conflict with management's estimate of "when" they can deliver. They then need to discuss resources and make decisions about how best to use the ones they have, and how they could get more.

Some organizations have started to distribute more authority to those who do the work. Each one takes on more responsibility to ensure they are doing the right job. Managers still set priorities and hold responsibility for ensuring everyone meets targets. Leading an organization like this can put the leader in closer contact with those who do the work. Working with these leaders may often inspire people in the organization to work harder and smarter.

When you decide to join an organization, consider the leadership and the management. If you are already in an organization, look at the decisions made by your managers and leadership. You likely will not know all the facts they face in making decisions, so you shouldn't try to second-guess their choices. Your factors for managers could be the degree to which they meet their targets and have the trust and support of their teams. In leadership, look for communication of vision, direction and passion for achievement. Lean towards opportunities to work with those who rank high in these factors. It is better to experience models of how to do things right. Examples of the other choice are more available, but not as helpful. Building experience of what to do to succeed and how to do it will help your decision-making abilities.

Secret Tip: **Choose to work with people who make good decisions.**

Chapter 10

Practice and Analysis

What was the last significant decision you made? It is often easier to see its significance when looking back. How would you rate its significance on a 1 to 10 scale? Would you have given it the same rating when you started to face that decision? If we can accurately gauge the significance of a decision when going into it, we have a better chance of making a good one.

By analysing past decisions, we can learn more about how to improve. Were you aware of the major risks and benefits the choices held, as you made the decision? Was your regard for them accurate? Were there any consequences that you did not foresee? Were you able to pursue resulting opportunities? How did you feel about the choice you finally made? Did it help you towards a goal? Was your final choice consistent with your values? How so?

This type of review and analysis is a healthy way to move

on after a major decision. Think about these questions instead of wondering if you could have done things differently. You could even write them out and put your answer after each one. It puts a final touch on your final decision. If you are not happy with your answers, use that to your advantage. Find part of your decision-making process that you need to improve. Mark it in your mind as something you should focus on for your next decision. Then be alert for a chance to practice your decision-making process again. Choose something that is not so critical.

This time, stall your process when you get to the part where you need to improve. Focus on the steps in that part. Take your time and become more familiar with it. Discuss it with someone you trust. Look for more options and use your imagination. Start putting numbers with your attitudes about the factors. Consider why you were not happy with your treatment of this part in your last decision. See if you have dealt properly with it this time. Continue your decision-making process and declare numbers for all the factors. Look at the numbers and think about your best choice. Talk it over with those you trust, if it makes you feel more comfortable. Make your decision and then act on it.

Practicing the Look Back

Do you want to make better decisions? Better than what? The best answer to this is, "Better than my previous decisions." But how will you know if your decision-making is getting better? You can tell by looking back on your significant decisions after you act on them. Remember the two points we mentioned in Chapter 1 about the quality of decisions. First, revealing the true merits of a decision requires you to carry out the decision. Second, a good decision helps to achieve a goal for the decision-maker.

So when analysing your recent decision, besides your review, consider these three questions. Did this decision achieve the results you hoped it would? Are you happy with the results of your decision? What could you have done better in preparing for the decision?

To make good decisions, you need to track the quality of decisions you make. These three questions will help you check your progress. Making good decisions is likely the best asset you could bring into your future. In fact, the quality of your future is depending on it.

Secret Tip: **Track the quality of your decisions.**

Secret Tip Summary

1.   Imagine how you would feel living with your decision in the future.

2.   You see the true merits of a decision after it is made.

3.   Clarify your goal before making a choice.

4.   Reflecting on a recent decision can help you improve future decisions.

5.   Start to simplify a decision by writing a list of possible choices.

6.   Label each risk so you can think and talk about it more easily with others.

7.   Chart your decision choices to make them clear to you and others.

8.   Investigate your situation's facts before asking the opinions of others.

9.   Seek help from knowledgeable people who are successful and share your values.

10.   Don't duck a decision when you would be better off making one.

11. Strengthen your decision framework by knowing your values and strategy.

12. Consider discarding choices that don't feel right or support your values or strategy.

13. Diagram your choices to get a visual impression.

14. Ask yourself questions about your decision as if it were your friend's.

15. Plan for what you expect, but also prepare yourself for the unexpected.

16. Try to decide quickly once you have asked other people to keep your confidence.

17. When choosing a goal, write a description of it and then make it even clearer.

18. Try to include the most important benefits on the path to your goal.

19. Prepare for consequences by planning for both avoidance and recovery.

20. Form an opinion on opportunities first, and then ask individuals for their advice.

21. When you are hoping for an opportunity, examine possible paths.

22. Try to make decisions before you must.

23. Learn to "listen" to your intuition.

24. Intuition works best in a familiar environment.

25.   Consider effects of your risks and consequences on others when likelihoods are high.

26.   A decision with high risk and big benefit justifies the time to get it right.

27.   Make your actions produce an intentional outcome.

28.   When you have decided the best way to do something, formalize it as a procedure.

29.   Choose to work with people who make good decisions.

30.   Track the quality of your decisions.

An Alternate Visual Model

The angle model is a simple tool to let you visualize risks and benefits. If you prefer to think in terms of rectangular models instead of angles, this alternative might interest you. It has some features that go a little deeper into the concept. Think of your risk as a square column that is always the same height for every situation. The bigger the risk, the more floor space the column takes for its square. For a risk of 10, the column is a cube. It is 10 units on each side on the floor, and it is always 10 units high. For a smaller risk, the column takes only a small square footprint, but is still 10 units high.

Let's use the example of Kayla we used earlier in the *Risks and Benefits* section of *Chapter 2: Understanding Decisions*. The numbers she used for her job offer choice appeared in *Figure 1*, but we can recall them here. For Kayla, the risk was five, as shown in *Figure 10*. The *likelihood* fills up the column to a maximum of 10. Kayla's

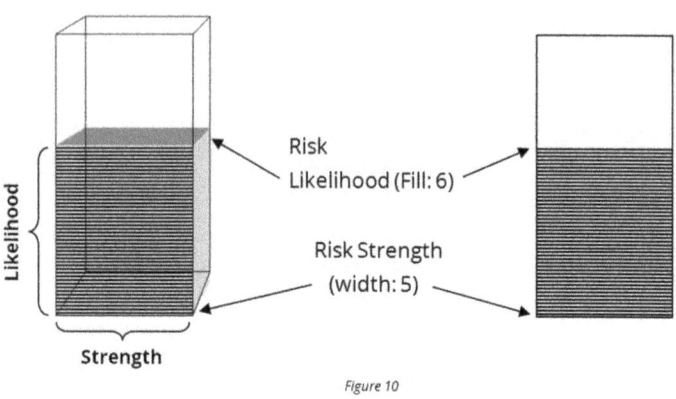

Risk
Likelihood (Fill: 6)

Risk Strength
(width: 5)

Likelihood

Strength

Figure 10

risk had a likelihood of six.

Looking at the column from the side, we only see the height and width of the column, and the amount of fill. This is a simplified way to see it. The width represents the strength of the risk, and the fill shows how likely it is. We could have a very narrow column that was full. That would show a very small risk that is certain to happen, like a small cost. We could also think of a huge risk that is quite unlikely. Our simplified view of it would show an almost empty square with a tiny amount of fill at the bottom.

Using this "building-block" way of visualizing the numbers for risk strength and likelihood, we can apply a similar visual to benefit. We use the width to represent the *strength* of risk or benefit, starting with the strongest. We show the strongest risk and the strongest benefit side-by-side, with the benefit to the right of the risk. This gives us our base.

Kayla's only risk was "miss home," and her biggest benefit was to "earn some $$." The left side of *Figure 11* shows these together. That benefit strength was 9, and the likelihood was 8. So, the benefit width at 9 would almost, but not quite, make a square. The likelihood at 8 would not fill up the square, but come near the top.

After drawing the strongest risk and benefit, we stack the others on top in descending order of strength. Kayla had only one risk, but she did have three benefits. If she had two more risks, we would see a sort of pyramid shape. The right side of *Figure 11* shows the risk and all the benefits for Kayla's choice.

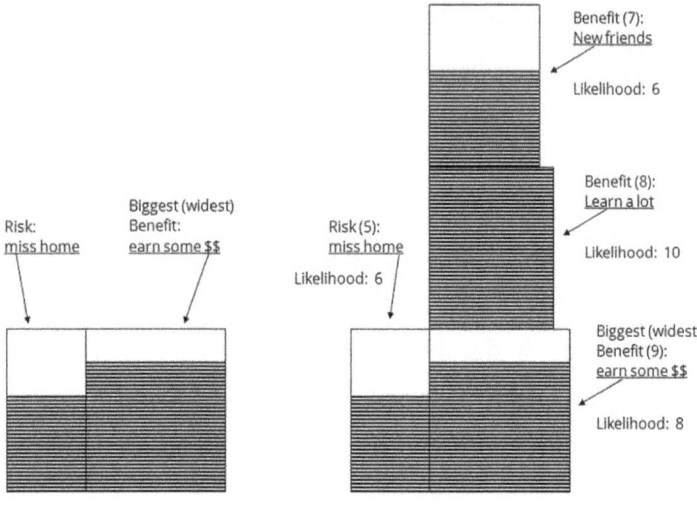

Figure 11

Just by glancing at the far right side of *Figure 11,* we can see this to be an outstanding choice for Kayla. She needs to compare it with her other choices, but this visual representation can help her do that.

A Foundation for Visual Building-Blocks

Foundation Factors work nicely into our visual building-block model. Let's look at them in the context of Terrence's bike purchase decision. We'll repeat the context here for convenience.

Terrence wants to get a bike to ride to school and work, and to use for fun on weekends. He has shopped around local stores and tried out a few bikes. The high-end bikes really appeal to him, with their light carbon frames and responsive handling. Unfortunately, they cost several times his available budget. He would have to borrow most of the money for a high-end bike. The bikes at the lower end of the price list are within his budget. They are heavier and handle a little more sluggishly, but they would be better than not having a bike.

Another option is to buy a used bike through an online ad. There he might be able to find a higher-end bike that he could afford. If he buys through a certain store he likes, he can use their scan and motion-capture bike fitting system as part of the deal. He is not a bike expert and is a little skeptical about buying a used bike from a stranger. To see his choices more clearly, Terrence used the decision framework to record his numbers. He found that he didn't see any opportunity differences between his choices, so he left that part out. *Figure 6* (repeated here) shows his assessment.

#	Choice	Risk	Strength	Likelihood	Consequence	Likelihood	Benefit	Strength	Likelihood	Feeling	Support for Values	Strategy
1	High end	Borrow $	8	10	Lose Bike	6	Easyride	7	10	6	8	8
2	Low end	Unhappy	5	4	Won't ride	4	Fit System	7	9	7	9	9
							Afford it	8	10			
3	Used	Worn out	7	6	Repair $$	7	Afford it	8	10	5	7	8

Figure 6

While the high-end bike is so attractive, Terrence is not sure he can afford it even with a loan. The payments would be large. Since his job is temporary, he wonders about his ability to pay back any loan over time. If he could not make the payments in the future, he would lose his bike. It is a great ride, but he has mixed feelings about it.

If he gets a bike that isn't as much fun for him, he worries that he may not ride it on weekends. A lower priced bike would be fine to get him to school and work, and he wouldn't feel the burden of payments. It fits his values and supports his need for transportation. He could also help ensure a good match by using the store's bike fitting system. The store is currently promoting it by including a fit with certain lower priced bikes.

He could get a high-end bike used, but he doesn't feel confident about knowing that it would not need repairs soon. He is not very familiar with high-end bikes and would have to find a way not to pay more than the bike is worth. Not one of his friends has a high-end bike. His goal is to get a bike he can use mainly for transportation, so the high-end part would just be for fun.

Let's see how his ratings appear in diagrams, shown in *Figure 12.*

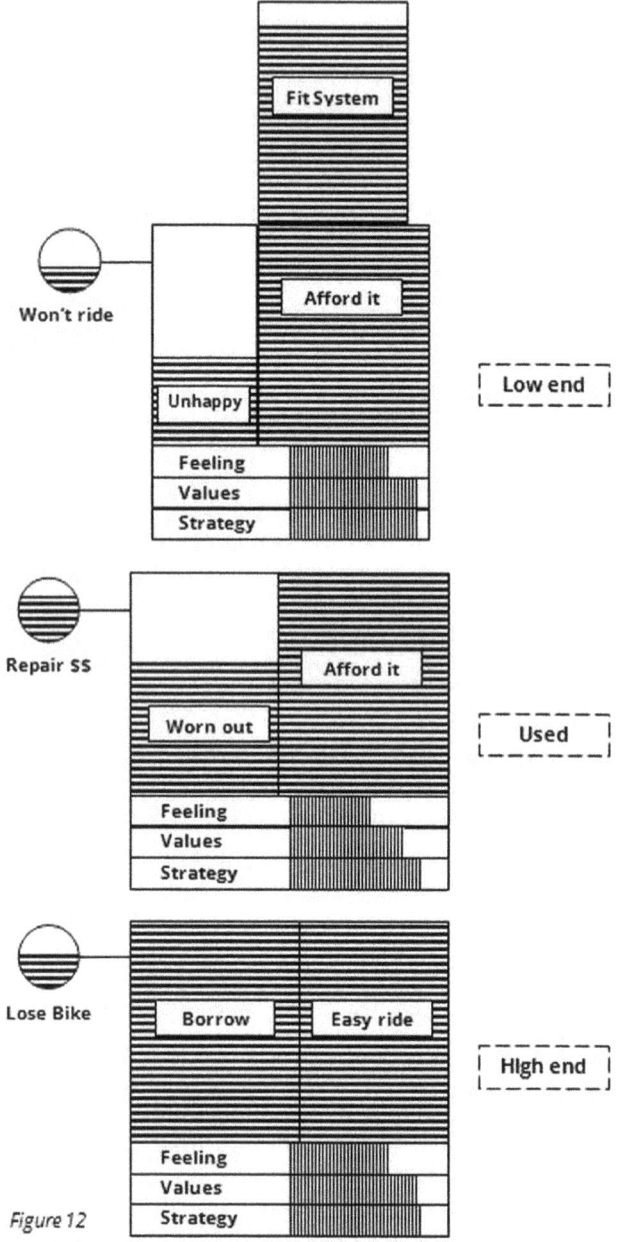

Figure 12

Interpreting the Diagrams

Looking at the diagrams in *Figure 12*, we see one diagram for each choice stacked on top of one another. A small gap separates them. The bottom choices have the widest base. It is the sum width of risk and benefit strength. The top choice has the least combination of risk and benefit. It is the most conservative choice. Here's one way to think about it. If the top choice had a width of only one unit for risk and one unit for benefit, would anyone care much about that choice? It would be very slim. Even if the likelihood for both the risk and the benefit were certain, the choice would not be upsetting or exciting.

Choices on the bottom are more major. Imagine a choice with a risk and benefit of ten units each. It would be the widest possible choice. Now fill them both with almost full likelihood. This is a stressful choice. The risks are huge and almost certain. But the benefit is also huge and almost certain. This kind of choice with such a big risk should have a benefit that contributes to your personal growth or development. That might make it a more attractive choice.

In Terrence's case, his High-end base shows a risk of eight and a benefit of seven. The width is 15 units out of a possible 20. This choice is somewhat stressful, but since both are certainties, he knows what to expect. Still, it is not attractive. The one consequence of the risk shows a good likelihood to lose the bike if he cannot make loan payments. That stress is all for an "easy ride" benefit. Terrence would say that it is a "beautiful" ride, since he took one of those bikes for a test ride at the store. It is impressive and Terrence is emotional about it, but his feelings are a little mixed. Let's look at those in more detail.

The Foundation Factors are at the bottom of each choice diagram. They expand sideways from the middle to show positive ratings to the right, and negative ratings to the left. Terrence's desire for a high-end bike shows in his Feeling score on this high-end choice. While excited, he is also feeling uncomfortable with such a big purchase price. It is far beyond what he can afford, or needs to spend. So he gave it a Feeling of six. He rated the consistency with his Values as eight because having this kind of bike would last him a lifetime. It would be an investment in his future, perhaps. That's what he told himself. He also gave an eight rating as support for his Strategy because the high-end bike would get him to school and work in fine style.

As you can see by the Foundation Factors in *Figure 12*, Terrence didn't feel as strongly about the used bike choice.

But buying a new lower-end bike did feel right to him. It also was much more consistent with his Values, since he would not have to carry any debt for it. He gave his Strategy support a higher rating for this choice than he did the others. He wanted a new bike that would be trouble-free and well suited to him. Given that the store promotion included the fitting system, this choice was better suited to his goal.

Since the Foundation Factors always extend from the middle of the base, it is easy to see whether risk or benefit is strongest. The boundary between the major risk and benefit will usually be to the left or right of the centre line. For Terrence's High-end choice, risk is wider and therefore stronger. Likelihoods are both certain. The other two choices have stronger benefits than risk. The likelihoods of their risk are less, as well. The top choice is for the low-end bike, showing an added benefit of the fit system with a strong likelihood. Even if Terrence is unhappy with this bike and wishes he were riding a high-end bike, the likelihood of that risk's consequence is low. We see consequences as circles connected by a line to their risk, filled with a degree of Likelihood. For example, the "won't ride" consequence circle connects to the left of the "Unhappy" risk. We see it filled not even halfway with likelihood, since Terrence rated it as a four. Terrence chose to buy the lower-end bike.

As we learned earlier, Terrence did not see special opportunities coming from any of the benefits. For the sake of discussion, let's pretend that the fitting system he saw at the store fascinated him. It appealed to him so much that he wondered if he could master it and perhaps get a job using it for customers at the store. If he bought a bike from the store, and learned all he could about the system, he might improve his chances of getting that job. How should we show that potential opportunity in relation to the Fit System benefit? *Figure 13* shows the New Job opportunity connected to the Fit System benefit.

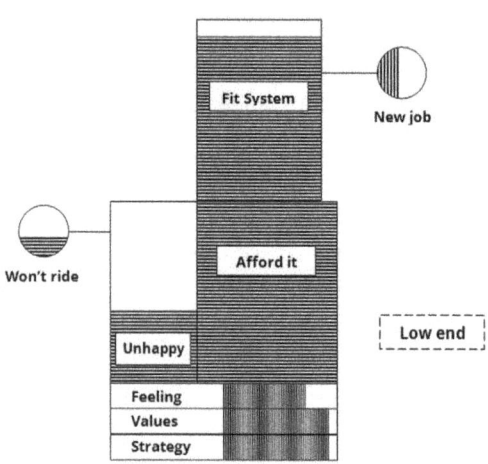

Figure 13

We rate the likelihood of the New Job opportunity happening at only four. If Terrence were to study it first and present himself as quite knowledgeable about it, we would raise that number. We show likelihoods for opportunities as fills of the circle, expanding from left to right. This way, we easily see them as different from the circles of consequences.

Showing Cost

We did not show cost in the diagrams for Terrence's decision. If we had, it would display as a thin column on top of the existing risk, with a full likelihood. For Terrence, his expenditure for the bike would be at least the same for all three choices. He had set aside a certain amount that he wanted to spend on the bike and he wanted to get the best bike he could for that money. He would spend that amount in any of the three choices. For the high-end bike, he would have to borrow money and spend more, but he would also spend the amount he had set aside. So the borrowed money shows as extra risk.

We show cost as a risk of full certainty, since we usually know the amount. The width, or strength, of the risk depends on the impact that spending will have on you.

Since Terrence had already set aside that amount of money for the bike, spending it would not impact him much at all. The width of that risk would be narrow. Because the risk was small and the same in all three choices, we did not show it in this example. We also wanted to introduce the diagram concept without extra clutter. If you wanted to be completely accurate, you could include the cost in the diagrams and the number chart. Usually, we leave out ratings that do not influence any of the choices.

Drawing the Diagrams

This section is to help you if you want to draw the diagrams. Feel free to skip over it if you have no interest in drawing them.

You can draw the diagrams as a sketch, a scale drawing, or imagined in your mind. After you have drawn a few, as either a sketch or a scale drawing, it becomes easier to draw them in your imagination. You might even skip the step of picking and recording numbers. You could visualize the diagram widths with fill levels directly from your knowledge of the situation. But drawing them can be fun, and it allows you to share them with others. Here are some guidelines that might help you draw them.

When you focus on drawing the shapes, it is nice not to have to recall the numbers. Writing the numbers in a chart lets you simply look them up when you need them. So, write the number chart first, as shown in *Figures 4, 5* or *6*. Draw a separate diagram for each choice to the same scale and stack them from bottom to top. Put the widest one at the bottom and thinnest at the top. Centre them using their bases as a reference, and leave a little gap between them. See *Figure 12* for an example.

To draw the diagram for a choice, start by measuring its base width. Work with risk and benefit first. Their combined width will never exceed 20 units. We add the strengths for risk and benefit together to get the total width of your base. Do this for the biggest risk and largest benefit in a choice, if there is more than one each in that choice. Also, do this for all choices to find the choice with the widest base. Start with that choice at the bottom. We are going to stack the choices, with the widest base shown at the bottom. The height for each risk or benefit will always be 10 units.

If you are drawing to scale, rather than just a sketch, choose your scale unit. For example, if you are using graph paper, decide how many squares make up a height of 10. If you use a ruler, you will be counting units. Decide how many tick marks make 10 or 20. On a computer, decide how many grid marks make 10 or 20. The easiest choice would be one mark stands for one unit. Use the same scale in both the vertical and horizontal directions. A 10 by 10 square should look square.

Draw the rectangle for risk on the left and for benefit on the right. They are both 10 units high. Fill the risk with horizontal lines for the risk likelihood number of units. Fill the benefit rectangle with horizontal lines up to the benefit likelihood number of units.

You may have another risk or benefit to add to this choice. If so, pick the risk and benefit combination that has the next widest total base. Draw the rectangles for risk and benefit so that the line they share between them aligns with the line below. Said another way, you should align all the benefit rectangles to the left in their stack. Align all the risk rectangles to the right in their stack. As an example, see how the Fit System benefit lines up with the Afford It benefit rectangle below it, in *Figure 12*. Fill the rectangles with their appropriate amount of likelihood. Continue with any remaining risk and benefit rectangles for this choice.

We are ready to add the Foundation Factors below the bottom risk and benefit rectangles. You will always have rectangles for Feeling and Values. You may also have one for Strategy if this choice relates to a goal. The Foundation Factor rectangles are always one unit high each. All three are always the same width as each other. That width can vary from choice to choice, but it is always the full width of the biggest risk and strongest benefit combined. Draw the Foundation Factor rectangles below the bottom risk and benefit rectangles.

You will need a new scale to calculate the fill amounts for the Foundation Factors. Start by finding the horizontal midpoint. That is the beginning of your fill amount. You are going to fill with vertical lines to the left for negative foundation numbers and to the right for positive numbers. To find the number of tick marks or grid lines, you will need a new scale factor. One simple way is to count the number of tick marks in the full width of your base and divide by 20. This is your foundation scale factor. Look at the Foundation Factor numbers in your chart. Multiply each number by this scale factor to get the number of tick marks for the fill. A Strategy number of 10, for example, would exactly fill that half of the rectangle. A value of five would be half way through that side. Count the number of tick marks or grids to see the extent of your fill.

When you stack all the choices on top of one another, all the beginning points of the foundation fills line up. You have seen this in *Figure 12*. This happens because you centre the diagrams for each choice horizontally on each other, like a pyramid. It helps to illustrate that the Foundation Factors for the choice at the top are not as wide as the ones are for the choice at the bottom. This makes sense when you think more about it. If you had a choice with a risk width of only one unit and a benefit of only one unit, it would be quite narrow. Even if you had a Feeling factor of 10 about that choice, the risk and benefit are so small that it hardly matters. The width of the fill for that Feeling factor would be quite small compared to Feeling factors for choices below it on the pyramid. This makes sense visually when looking at several choices together.

We draw consequences and opportunities as circles connected by a line to their respective risk or benefit. Vertical fills show likelihoods of consequences from the bottom up. Horizontal fills show likelihoods of opportunities from the left towards the right. See *Figure 13* for reference. These fills do not need accurate measurement. We draw them simply to show approximations of the likelihoods. A fully filled circle represents 10; half full is five. Just represent other numbers as best as you can.

If you are using a computer for drawing, you can use a trick to draw these more easily. Create two circles of the same size. One is empty (transparent) inside its circular border. Fill the other with the appropriate fill pattern, but give it no border. Place it behind (layered under, in the third dimension) the first circle, and centre them on each other. It now looks like you have a circle filled with the pattern. Place a white-filled square with no border in a layer between the two circles. Now adjust the width or height of the white square to reveal just the amount of fill you need. Since the white square is in a layer between the two circles, it blocks out the part of the fill pattern that it covers. The round circle border on the top layer is always visible. Group these objects to move and size them together.

Understanding Strength and Likelihood

You may come across some unusual combinations of risk and benefit that have opposite likelihoods. We see two extreme examples of risk and benefit in *Figure 14*.

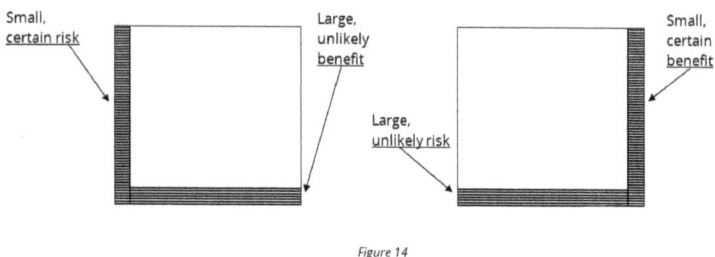

Figure 14

On the left side we see a small but certain risk, like a payment, along with a large benefit. While the benefit is potentially quite large, it is unlikely. An example of this choice could be buying a lottery ticket.

On the right side, we see a very large risk that is unlikely, along with a small but certain benefit. An example of this could be a dare to do something risky and unfamiliar. The benefit is to preserve your pride. The dare could be to dive off the high platform into a pool for the first time. It is unlikely you will be injured, but if you are it could change your life.

In both these cases, we have shown the thickness as one unit on the diagram. (For real life situations, the number may be only a fraction of one.) On the left, we have one unit of certain risk strength with one unit of benefit likelihood. On the right, we have one unit of risk likelihood with one unit of certain benefit strength. We have nicknamed these types of choices "L's" and "J's," inspired by their appearance. L's are "Low-risk" choices with a sketchy benefit. J's are "Just-risk" (as in mainly risk) choices because there is so little benefit, and a chance of disaster. L's can be fun, as long as you won't feel too disappointed if it doesn't work out. J's are choices of daredevils, or of friends you might call foolish or stupid. Another example of a J choice is getting a ride home with a drinking driver. If you are lucky, you may get home safely, but it will be a tragedy otherwise. Both L and J choices involve chance, but with very different stakes. If you beat the odds with an L choice, things are great. Beating the odds in a J choice can be the worst day of your life.

These "close to the edge" cases may appear hard to compare to each other. Just looking at the diagrams, you might think that they were equally significant. The shaded areas look to be about the same. Yet, you know that buying a lottery ticket is not the same significance as a novice diving off the high platform into a pool. So, how do we sort out the significance of these two situations?

Remember that in *Figure 10* we introduced risk as a square column, filled to a point with likelihood. We have mainly been looking at the columns from just a side view. If we were to take the L choice of the lottery ticket example and move it over to view at an angle, it would appear as in *Figure 15.*

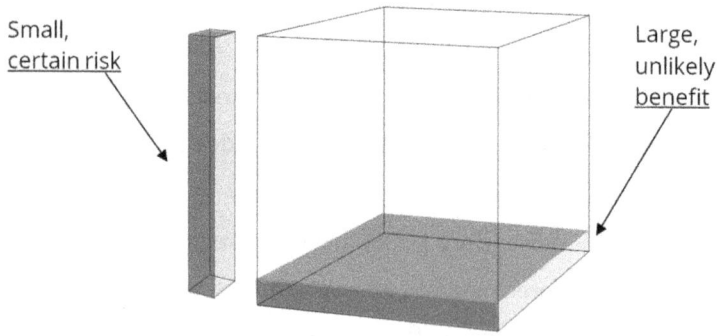

Small, certain risk

Large, unlikely benefit

Figure 15

We see the two square-footprint columns for risk and benefit. Their likelihood fills them to different levels. It is now clear that the benefit is more significant than the risk in this L choice. The risk column could fall over next to the benefit's likelihood and not begin to hide it. The certain risk is much smaller than the unlikely benefit. The same concept applies to J choices, but risk is the large low part. For J choices, the certain benefit is much smaller than an unlikely risk. Said another way, for J choices, the unlikely risk is much larger than the certain benefit.

When we look at just a side view, as in *Figure 14*, it we might believe that a strength is just as significant as a likelihood. When we view or imagine L and J choices in the 3D view, it gives us new perspective. It reminds us that the **strength** of a risk or a benefit is far more significant than its likelihood. The 3D view of *Figure 15* lets us see that strengths have a lot more behind them. A large unlikely risk or benefit will have a huge impact if it does happen. There is a chance it will change everything, even though it may be slim. This 3D view helps persuade us of that important fact.

Once you understand your own position on a decision, you may want to explain it to others. Having more than one visualization tool can sometimes be helpful in doing that. This building-block model, with its 3D view option, is now available to you if you need it.

Works Cited

Alex Lowey, P. H. (2004). *The Power of the 2x2 Matrix.* San Fransisco: Jossey-Bass / Wiley.

Chamorro-Premuzic, T. (2013). *Confidence: Overcoming Low Self-Esteem, Insecurity, and Self-Doubt.* New York: Hudson Street Press, a Penguin Random House Company.

Government of Canada. (1982). CONSTITUTION ACT, 1982. *Part I, Section 7.* Ottawa, Canada. Retrieved from http://laws-lois.justice.gc.ca/eng/const/page-15.html

Jeffers, S. (2006). Feel the Fear and Do It Anyway®: Dynamic techniques for turning Fear, Indecision and Anger into Power, Action and Love. New York: Fawcett, The Random House Publishing Group.

Kahneman, D. (2011). *Thinking, Fast and Slow.* New York: Farrar, Straus and Giroux.

Kurzweil, R. (2012). *How to Create a Mind: The Secret of Human Thought Revealed.* London, England: VIKING The Penguin Group.

Paul O'Brien, J. G. (2015). *Great Decisions, Perfect Timing: Cultivating Intuitive Intelligence.* Portland OR: Divination Foundation Press.

Robert S. Kaplan, D. P. (1996). *The Balanced Scorecard: translating strategy into action.* Boston: Harvard Business School Press.

Also see SecretsOfDecisionIsland.com

About the Author

Over 30 years in high technology, Tom Berryhill has hired and worked with many young people while achieving significant accomplishments. Throughout his career he has encouraged seeing issues objectively from differing perspectives, while honouring attitudes and feelings. His experience in corporate management, for public and private companies, has required him to explain important concepts in ways that are easy to grasp. By combining innovation and strategic thinking, he enjoys helping others make important decisions confidently. He now focuses that experience for those wanting to make good decisions in their life.

Lightning Source UK Ltd.
Milton Keynes UK
UKHW02f1037100718
325485UK00015B/1015/P

9 780994 807137